best
hikes
with
dogs
BAY AREA & BEYOND

best hikes with dogs
BAY AREA & BEYOND

Thom Gabrukiewicz

THE MOUNTAINEERS BOOKS

THE MOUNTAINEERS BOOKS
is the nonprofit publishing arm of The Mountaineers Club, an organization founded in 1906 and dedicated to the exploration, preservation, and enjoyment of outdoor and wilderness areas.

1001 SW Klickitat Way, Suite 201, Seattle, WA 98134

© 2004 by Thom Gabrukiewicz
All rights reserved

First edition: First printing 2004, second printing 2006, third printing 2007

No part of this book may be reproduced in any form, or by any electronic, mechanical, or other means, without permission in writing from the publisher.

Published simultaneously in Great Britain by Cordee, 3a DeMontfort Street, Leicester, England, LE1 7HD

Manufactured in the United States of America

Acquiring Editor: Laura Drury
Project Editor: Laura Drury
Copy Editor: Julie Van Pelt
Cover and Book Design: The Mountaineers Books
Layout Artist: Ani Rucki
Cartographer: Pease Press Custom Cartography
All photographs by the author unless otherwise noted.
Cover photograph: *Trinity.* Photo by Michael Burke
Frontispiece: *Life's a beach when you take your canine companion with you and your family on the trails of Northern California.*

Library of Congress Cataloging-in-Publication Data
Gabrukiewicz, Thom.
  Best hikes with dogs : Bay Area and beyond / by Thom Gabrukiewicz.— 1st ed.
    p.   cm.
  Includes bibliographical resources and index.
  ISBN 0-89886-757-6
  1. Hiking with dogs—California—San Francisco Region—Guidebooks. 2. San Francisco Region (Calif.)—Guidebooks. I. Title.
  SF427.455.G24 2004
  796.51'09794'6—dc22
                                    2004023956

ISBN 10: 0-89886-757-6
ISBN 13: 978-0-89886-757-2

CONTENTS

Trinity sticks to the trail, through Bort Meadows in the Chabot Regional Park near Oakland.

HIKE SUMMARY TABLE

Trail	Easy on paws	Easy hike, about 4 miles	Overnight	Water for swimming	Unleashed OK	Solitude	Alpine scenery	Forested	Good for senior dogs	For fit dogs
Shasta-Cascade										
1 PCT to Seven Lakes Basin			•	•	•	•	•	•		•
2 Castle and Heart Lakes		•	•	•	•		•	•		•
3 Squaw Valley Creek Trail	•			•	•	•		•	•	
4 McCloud Waterfalls	•	•	•	•	•	•		•	•	
5 Mount Eddy and Deadfall Lakes			•	•	•	•	•	•		•
6 Castle Dome							•	•		•
7 Bailey Cove Loop	•	•		•	•			•		
8 Waters Gulch Creek to Packers Bay	•			•	•	•		•	•	
9 Clikapudi Trail	•			•				•	•	
10 Boulder Creek Falls	•		•	•	•			•	•	
11 Mill Creek Trail	•			•	•	•		•	•	
12 Davis Gulch Trail	•			•	•		•	•	•	
13 Kanaka Peak				•	•	•	•	•		•
14 Arboretum Perimeter Trail	•	•		•				•		
15 Sacramento River Trail	•			•				•		
16 Blue Gravel Mine Trail	•	•						•		
17 Magee Peak			•	•	•		•	•		•
18 Baker Lake to Hat Creek Rim	•			•	•					•
19 Crystal and Baum Lakes	•			•	•				•	
20 Hat Creek Trail	•		•	•	•		•	•	•	
21 Caribou Wilderness Area	•		•	•	•	•	•	•	•	
22 McGowan Lake Trail	•	•		•	•		•	•	•	
23 Lake Almanor Recreation Trail	•				•		•	•	•	
24 Bizz Johnson Trail	•		•	•	•	•		•		

Trail	Easy on paws	Easy hike, about 4 miles	Overnight	Water for swimming	Unleashed OK	Solitude	Alpine scenery	Forested	Good for senior dogs	For fit dogs
Sacramento and the Gold Country										
25 South Yuba Independence Trail	•			•	•				•	
26 Bullards Bar Trail	•		•	•	•			•	•	
27 Codfish Creek Trail	•	•		•	•	•			•	
28 American River Parkway	•			•					•	
29 Summit Lake Trail	•	•	•	•	•		•		•	
30 Folsom Lake and Mormon Island Dam	•		•	•	•		•		•	
31 Loch Leven Lakes	•		•	•	•	•	•	•		•
32 Caples Lake to Emigrant Lake	•		•	•	•		•	•		•
33 Lake Margaret	•		•	•	•	•	•	•	•	
34 Crooked Lakes Trail to Penner Lake	•		•	•	•		•	•		•
San Francisco Bay Area										
35 South Beach Trail		•		•	•	•			•	
36 Bolinas Ridge	•					•		•		•
37 Barnabe Peak	•			•	•	•				•
38 Roys Redwoods Trail	•	•			•			•	•	
39 San Geronimo Ridge	•				•	•				•
40 Cascade Falls Trail	•	•		•	•		•	•	•	
41 Alpine Lake Trail	•			•	•	•	•	•		•
42 Two Lakes Trail	•			•			•	•		•
43 Cataract Falls and Laurel Dell				•				•		•
44 Mount Tamalpais East Peak Trail				•				•		•
45 Pine Mountain Summit					•	•				•
46 Phoenix Lake	•	•		•					•	
47 Deer Island	•	•			•	•			•	•
48 Mount Burdell	•				•	•		•		•

Trail	Easy on paws	Easy hike, about 4 miles	Overnight	Water for swimming	Unleashed OK	Solitude	Alpine scenery	Forested	Good for senior dogs	For fit dogs
49 Waterfall Trail and Indian Valley	•	•		•	•			•		
50 Ring Mountain	•	•			•			•	•	
51 Blithedale Ridge	•				•	•				•
52 Rodeo Lagoon	•	•		•					•	
53 Miwok and Bobcat Trails	•					•				•
54 Fort Baker	•	•				•			•	
55 Golden Gate Promenade	•								•	
56 Sweeney Ridge	•	•				•				•
57 Fort Funston Sunset Trail	•	•							•	
58 Ocean Beach Esplanade	•			•	•				•	
59 Rockaway Point	•	•		•	•				•	
60 Gray Whale Cove	•	•			•				•	
61 San Pedro Mountain	•					•				•
62 Pulgas Ridge	•	•							•	
63 Arastradero Preserve	•	•							•	
64 Anthony Chabot Loop	•				•			•	•	
65 Bort Meadow	•				•	•		•		•
66 West Ridge Loop	•	•						•	•	
67 Sibley Volcanic Regional Preserve	•	•			•			•	•	
68 Nimitz Way	•								•	
69 San Pablo Ridge Trail	•					•			•	
70 Laurel Loop	•	•						•	•	
71 Sobrante Ridge Trail	•	•			•	•			•	
72 Briones Crest	•				•					•
73 Lafayette Ridge	•				•	•				•
74 Franklin Ridge	•				•	•				•
75 Murietta Falls					•	•				•

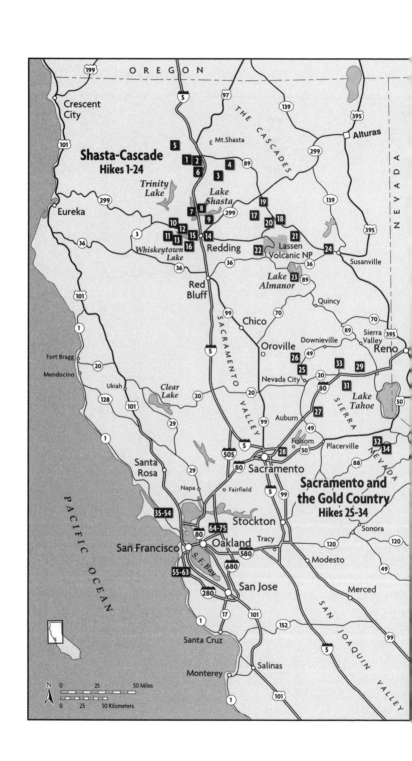

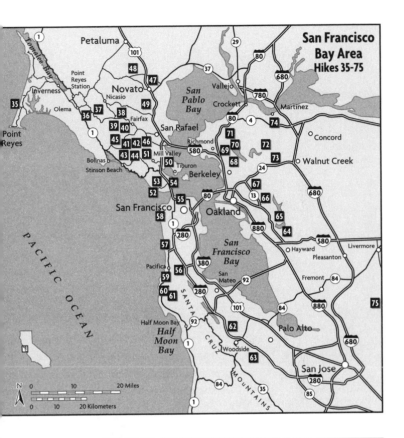

San Francisco Bay Area
Hikes 35–75

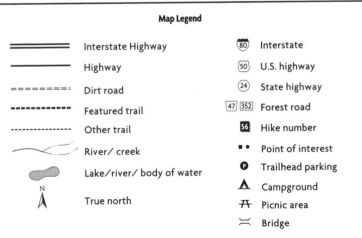

Map Legend

═════	Interstate Highway
────	Highway
════════	Dirt road
▪▪▪▪▪▪▪	Featured trail
┈┈┈┈┈	Other trail
∽∽	River/ creek
⬭	Lake/river/ body of water
⋏ N	True north

(80)	Interstate
(50)	U.S. highway
(24)	State highway
47 352	Forest road
56	Hike number
▪ •	Point of interest
℗	Trailhead parking
⛰	Campground
卅	Picnic area
⌣	Bridge

From several trails around the San Francisco Bay Area, the Golden Gate Bridge commands a hiker's attention.

AUTHOR'S NOTE

The day I was chosen to write this book, I could bend my right knee—with the aid of a device called the continuous passive motion machine—70 degrees. With terrific pain. Normally, people can bend their knees to 120 degrees, but a month before, I'd had arthroscopic surgery.

I am forty-two years old; the doctor said I had the knees of a sixty-year-old. I have degenerative joint disease, a hereditary condition that has entered me into a very noninclusive club—the 2.1 million Americans who suffer from rheumatoid arthritis. Within twenty years, I will have to go back into surgery and get the ailing knee replaced with components made of titanium and space-age ceramics.

So much for the lifestyle I had lived for most of my life—running, skiing, hiking, paddling, rock climbing, mountain biking, backpacking, and snowshoeing.

Or so I thought.

"You're cleared to resume normal activities, but let your conscience be your guide," the shocked orthopedic surgeon said four months after my surgery (I was a fiend during physical therapy). "One word of advice, though. I know backpacking and hiking are very important to you. You just can't be toting around loads of 40 and 50 pounds anymore, your knee can't take it. You have a dog, right? Heck, let him carry some of the load."

What luck! I have two dogs, Scully, a seven-year-old Australian shepherd/chow cross and Trinity, a four-year-old border collie cross. With their own packs, and some additional training, I figured I could cut my load down to 25 pounds or less—as long as I packed their items in sealed plastic bags. Pack or no pack, Trinity and Scully have never passed up an opportunity to frolic in a mountain stream, river, waterfall pool, muddy bog, or alpine lake.

The girls, as we like to call them, are blessedly good hikers. Through years of voice-command training, they can hike off-leash on most trails. This doesn't mean I leave the leashes in the truck. Whether dogs

The girls, Scully, left, and Trinity take a break during a dayhike to Boulder Creek Falls in Whiskeytown National Recreation Area.

are well behaved or not, many people don't like to share their open spaces with four-legged wanderers of the *Canine domesticus* variety.

Case in point: while traversing the rugged Lost Coast Trail from the mouth of the Mattole River to the community of Shelter Cove in Northern California, I was greeted one evening by a rather large Doberman named Coco (I learned her name as her owners cajoled her to behave). Coco had the habit of greeting a new person by shoving her muzzle in that person's crotch. Coco weighed at least 80 pounds, and also liked to growl in menacing, albeit muffled, tones.

The young couple assured me that Coco was harmless (in *that* position, who was I to argue?) as they hauled her away by the collar. They had no leash with them as restraint, as Coco proved by visiting our camp several times that evening.

I am not afraid of dogs. I do, however, dislike misbehaving mutts.

With that in mind, I decided to write a guide that people and their canine companions can use to find the places in Northern California that are dog-friendly. Places where people and dogs can find solitude, blazing displays of wildflowers, fishing opportunities, ample swimming, great views—and people of like persuasion, namely dog lovers.

This guide also became the best physical therapy a person could ever hope for. Walking and hiking are not only good for the soul, they are great for the body.

"A brisk walk can burn up to 100 calories per mile or 300 calories per hour," according to the American Podiatric Medical Association (*www.apma.org*). They continue, saying, "Walking is the perfect complement to a sensible diet to lose weight and keep it off.

"Walking improves cardiovascular fitness. As an aerobic exercise, walking gets the heart beating faster to transport oxygen-rich blood from the lungs to the muscles. The heart and lungs grow more efficient with a regular walking regimen, reducing blood pressure and the resting heart rate. Walking is even a central element of medical rehabilitation. Recovery from many ailments, including heart attack, is facilitated by a regular walking regimen."

So here's to health and here's to dogs, and sharing a trail (safely and sanely) to some of the most beautiful places in California.

PREFACE

Fifty-five million homeowners in the United States can't be wrong.

That's the number of Americans who have at least one dog or cat living with them, according to the Pet Food Institute (*petfoodinstitute.com*). There are an estimated 60 million dogs in the United States, and a Gallup poll showed that 50 percent of California households have dogs—an estimated 5,751,435, according to U.S. Census Bureau information for the year 2002.

We are a state that has gone to the dogs, and we want to share our open lands with our four-legged friends. Indeed, several high-population counties have dog political action committees to help plan open spaces for multiple use.

In Northern California, we are blessed with space—from national forests and regional parks to U.S. Bureau of Land Management lands and state parks. Still, the presence of canine companions on the trail continues to be a contentious situation. There are those who advocate no dogs on trails. Some groups contend that dogs don't belong in the wilderness, since they chase wildlife, harass other hikers, and foul trails and campsites. It's up to dog owners to soothe the fears of this small segment of the hiking population, with education—and with good trail manners.

There is a huge segment of the population who fears dogs. And any sort of trail encounter—even just your dog running up to a hiker to say hello—can be trouble. It's up to dog owners to be good stewards for all 5 million dog-owning households in California. Training goes a long way, as does a stout leash.

The question remains, however, "Are dogs harmful to the backcountry?" To that, I say, "No more than human wanderers."

Just as there are irresponsible hikers who cut switchbacks, camp too close to water sources, and don't bury their waste, there are problem dogs who have no business being on-trail. Sadly, this is a symptom of poor training. Even if you have voice and hand control of your dog, please always hike with a leash or harness.

Basically, dogs should adhere to the same backcountry ethics as their human masters. Dogs need to defecate at least 200 feet from a water source and the waste should be buried in a cat hole from 6 to 8 inches deep. Dogs shouldn't be allowed to cut a switchback. Dogs should never be encouraged to chase wildlife. Done right, dogs on trails can actually help hikers see more wildlife, since their senses of smell, sight, and hearing are superior to ours. That's been my experience with dogs on the trail—in fact, that's why there are so many dog breeds, each one created to increase the likelihood of seeing wildlife during a hunt.

But not all dog owners should just rush out and hit the trail. First, you need to know where dogs are allowed and where they are not. Most national parks and monuments allow dogs to enter, but trails are off-limits, even for the best-trained dog. Know the laws and land management rules governing each area you intend to visit with your canine companion, whether your destination is a state park or a national forest.

Each hike in this book allows dogs to share the trail. However, trail regulations can change from year to year because of conditions and new regulations. Hikers should always call the land manager to find out the current trail regulations and the current trail conditions of any new route.

Hikers also need to be aware of changing weather conditions and be prepared for anything. You can easily twist an ankle or jam a wrist crossing loose talus, and you may need to stay the night while waiting for an able-bodied hiker to walk out and summon help. Dogs also need care and tending: they can tear up their pads, fall off a slope, or get too close to some wildlife and get injured.

It all comes down to being prepared. An enjoyable time on your public lands depends on both you and your dog being ready not only for the elements, but for dispelling the myth that dogs cause havoc on the trail.

PART 1

Hiking with Your Dog

Packing up your dog and hitting the trail seems like a carefree, easy outing. But there are some things to consider, and preparations to make, before setting out. The following will help you and your dog stay safe and will go a long way toward making sure that you both have a good time—and that you don't affect the good time of other trail users.

Good Dogs Require Good Owners and Training

Think about how many hours of enjoyment and amusement your dog brings. Now think about the amount of training it takes to transform a mischievous puppy into a well-behaved older dog. Well-behaved pets are a direct reflection of their owners. Too often, pets are made to suffer for the sins of the master—and they often bear the brunt of any negative feelings generated by an irresponsible pet owner.

It seems strange that certain pet owners can't even meet the basic responsibilities of pet ownership—caring for a dog, feeding him, and keeping him healthy. You must also be responsible for your dog's exercise and recreation. Despite the 100,000 years since man first domesticated wolves, your dog still has a basic, wild need to run, jump, and swim.

It all begins with training.

I tend to believe that there are many more bad owners than there are "bad" breeds of dogs. However, there are those breeds that have been bred to bring out aggressive behavior. Consider this when selecting a new puppy or if you're about to adopt an older dog from a rescue organization or shelter. Internet research can lead you to basic breed traits that you can expect from your dog—even if that dog is a mixed breed.

Next step: work with your dog, daily if he or she is a puppy and weekly for an older dog. The first commands of sit, shake, stay, and lie down form the foundation of a "well-heeled" pet.

Most communities have dog-training classes, either through the parks and recreation department, community college, or some of the larger chain pet stores. Take a class. And back that training up with even more training. One of the better Internet sites for dog training comes from the University of Wisconsin–Stevens Point. Dr. P's Dog Training (*www.uwsp.edu/psych/dog/dog.htm*) is packed with information.

Another important component is "socializing" your dog with other dogs—and people. Take your pet to places where there are other dogs playing. Get your puppy used to crowds of people.

All such efforts allow your pet to be a popular fixture along the trail, since a well-trained dog is a delight to encounter.

Happy, Healthy Trails

Even responsible pet owners can have trouble realizing their dogs aren't invincible bundles of muscle and energy. While I was recuperating from knee surgery, my own dogs were left with nothing more than running around the yard for the ten weeks that I couldn't bear weight on my mangled knee. First hike out, both dogs cut their pads, and I had to carry Scully out on top of my pack—8 miles with an extra 50 pounds on my back. (Don't tell my doctor.)

Dogs that do nothing but lie in the living room or the backyard all day cannot be expected to challenge steep grades, gravel paths, and mountain trails without some ill effects. Like a human couch potato, dogs can get stiff, sore muscles, bruised and blistered toes, and all sorts of scrapes and bug bites.

To avoid this, you and your dog must stay active. Nothing extreme is required: just 30 minutes of walking a day does your body good, and that of your dog. As with any new exercise program, start gradually and build slowly. After a few weeks of walking, try running for 10 to 15 minutes, or quicken your walking pace.

This will help build muscle tone in both you and your pet, but more importantly, exercise will help toughen the pads on your dog's feet, making them ready to go off-road when you are. Those first hikes are where

Trinity follows the trail in the Golden Gate National Recreation Area near San Francisco.

you should go slow. Make your first several outings day hikes, on paved trails where you can get your dog used to hiking and to what's expected on the trail. Just as a good pair of hiking boots is essential for a positive backcountry experience, your dog's pads need to be in their best condition. There are pad-toughening agents for sale, but nothing beats good, clean exercise.

If you are partial to more-extreme hikes farther in the backcountry, I recommend you buy your dog a set of booties. There are several brands—and styles—on the market; with a little training, your dog will get used to—and even excited by—you pulling out the booties for a hike.

Also, remember that your dog can get stiff and sore after a day of hiking. Trying to get a sore dog to move out of camp after a day of rigorous hiking can be a chore. You either have to poke, prod, or resort to carrying your dog to get her moving. Some simple medications, like ordinary aspirin, can help. These are covered in detail under Canine First Aid later in the introduction.

What to Expect from Your Breed

On-trail, I've seen perky Pomeranians and lackadaisical Labradors, bulletlike border collies and plodding poodles. A good trail companion, it seems, depends more on training than breeding.

Trinity and Scully take a rest along the Seven Lakes Basin Trail with Mount Shasta as a backdrop.

With that said, you're probably going to get more miles out of a golden retriever than a Chihuahua. Some breeds, like dachshunds and bassets, can't carry packs, since they are built so close to the ground.

The best advice is to pick a breed that fits your lifestyle. If you plan on taking your dog with you often into the backcountry, a working breed, sporting breed, or something from the herding group will make a better companion than a dog from the toy group.

I fully believe in a dog carrying his or her own supplies. In talking to several veterinarians, I've found that dogs can carry a third of their body weight. Generally, my own dogs carry about 20 percent, including their food and treats, collapsible bowls for food and water, their first-aid kit, and the leashes. Puppies can't carry any weight until their bones finish growing. In some breeds, this can take up to two years. But do get your puppy used to a pack. Let her carry it empty around the yard. That way, when the time comes to get into the backcountry, your dog isn't going to try to buck the pack like a miniature bull.

Other considerations include a vest or sweater for short-haired breeds that can get cold in the backcountry.

Permits and Regulations

Simply put, know the rules and regulations of the areas where you plan to hike. Dogs are not allowed past the parking lots of national parks and monuments. Some regional parks allow dogs, but with certain restrictions (like leashes). Some only require that you have voice or hand control over your dog. Generally, national forests, wilderness areas (unless they are in national parks), and Bureau of Land Management (BLM) lands have no restrictions on bringing your dog with you to hike.

There are other, not necessarily dog-specific considerations, though.

If you plan on camping and on building a fire, you'll need to carry a free campfire permit—and know whether or not certain fire restrictions are in place, especially when it's dry. Fire permits can be picked up at national forest headquarters, ranger districts, and BLM offices. They are good for six months.

Some wilderness areas require that you carry a backcountry camping permit. Again, these free permits can be picked up at ranger district offices.

So far, most Northern California national forests don't require the so-called Adventure Pass to recreate (except for Lake Shasta and the Mount Shasta Wilderness Area). The $5-a-day pass ($30 a year) is required at Los Padres, Angeles, San Bernardino, and Cleveland National Forests in Southern

California and selected locations in Washington and Oregon. California has nineteen national forests that encompass 20 million acres.

However, support for the Adventure Pass continues to wane. The program was started in 1996 as a way to maintain and improve recreational facilities in the wake of constant budget cuts. Congress has considered making the program permanent, but Senator Barbara Boxer (D-CA) has come out against the pass altogether. This will be an issue well worth watching develop.

Leave No Trace

The Leave No Trace principles of outdoor ethics are paramount (see *www.leavenotrace.org*):

- Plan ahead and prepare.
- Travel and camp on durable surfaces.
- Dispose of waste properly.
- Leave what you find.
- Minimize campfire impacts.
- Respect wildlife.
- Be considerate of other visitors.

Plan Ahead and Prepare

Know the regulations and special concerns for the area you'll visit.

Prepare for extreme weather, hazards, and emergencies.

Schedule your trip to avoid times of high use.

Visit in small groups. Split larger parties into groups of four to six.

Repackage food to minimize waste.

Use a map and compass to eliminate the use of marking paint, rock cairns, or flagging.

Travel and Camp on Durable Surfaces

Durable surfaces include established trails and campsites, rock, gravel, dry grasses, and snow.

Protect riparian areas by camping at least 200 feet from lakes and streams.

Good campsites are found, not made. Altering a site is not necessary.

In popular areas: concentrate use on existing trails and campsites; walk single file in the middle of the trail, even when wet or muddy; keep campsites small; focus activity in areas where vegetation is absent.

In pristine areas: disperse use to prevent the creation of campsites and trails; avoid places where impacts are just beginning.

Dispose of Waste Properly

Pack it in, pack it out. Inspect your campsite and rest areas for trash or spilled foods. Pack out all trash, leftover food, and litter.

Deposit solid human waste in cat holes dug 6 to 8 inches deep at least 200 feet from water, camp, and trails. Cover the cat hole when finished.

Pack out toilet paper and hygiene products.

Carry wash water 200 feet away from streams or lakes and use small amounts of biodegradable soap. Scatter strained dishwater.

Leave What You Find

Preserve the past: examine, but don't touch, cultural or historic structures and artifacts.

Leave rocks, plants, and other natural objects as you find them.

Avoid introducing or transporting nonnative species.

Don't build structures or furniture, or dig trenches.

Minimize Campfire Impacts

Campfires can cause lasting impacts to the backcountry. Use a lightweight stove for cooking and enjoy a candle lantern for light.

Where fires are permitted, use established fire rings, fire pans, or mound fires.

Keep fires small. Only use sticks from the ground that can be broken by hand.

Burn all wood and coals to ash, put out campfires completely, then scatter cool ashes.

Respect Wildlife

Observe wildlife from a distance. Don't follow or approach animals.

Never feed animals. Feeding wildlife damages their health, alters natural behaviors, and exposes them to predators and other dangers.

This garter snake is one of nature's creatures you're likely to encounter in northern California.

Protect wildlife and your food by storing rations and trash securely.

Control pets at all times, or leave them at home.

Avoid wildlife during sensitive times: mating, nesting, raising young, or winter.

Be Considerate of Other Visitors

Respect other visitors and protect the quality of their experience.

Be courteous. Yield to other users on the trail.

Step to the downhill side of the trail when encountering pack stock.

Take breaks and camp away from trails and other visitors.

Let nature's sounds prevail. Avoid loud voices and noises.

Trail Etiquette for Dogs

Just as it's important for humans to follow Leave No Trace ethics, it's important that your dog—and you—follow a standard of trail etiquette. As a hiker, you are responsible for your actions; as a dog owner, you are also responsible for your dog's actions.

The hard-and-fast rule is to observe common sense and common courtesy. Here are some other rules to live by on the trail:

- Have your pet on a leash or under strict voice command at all times. Strict voice command means that your dog heels immediately when

Rest breaks are essential to hiking, as Trinity and Scully know. Here, they're perched on a bench during a rest stop on the Davis Gulch Trail.

told, stays at heel, and refrains from barking.

- When you and your dog meet other trail users, you should yield the right-of-way, stepping well clear of the trail to allow the other users to pass without problem.
- When you and your dog meet a mountain biker or horse, you should yield, and make sure your dog stays calm and under strict control. Stay off the trail—with a firm grasp on your dog—until the horse or biker is well clear of the area.
- When you meet other hikers, the group heading uphill has the right-of-way. It's much easier for descending hikers to break stride and find a safe place to step off the trail.
- Always stay on-trail and never make, or take, shortcuts. This leads to erosion. If your destination is off-trail, take the most direct route possible, as in leaving the trail in a perpendicular manner.
- Obey all rules and regulations for the trail on which you'll be hiking. Many trails are closed to certain uses, and kiosks at the trailhead will outline the rules.
- Avoid disturbing wildlife, period.
- Never roll rocks or logs downhill. You never know what—or who—is below you.

Canine First Aid

Dogs make lousy patients. Not only can't they tell you where it hurts, but they'll troop on forever with an injury, just because the sights and smells in the outdoors are so delicious. But with a height that's right about grass level, and a penchant for keeping their noses to the ground, dogs can run into all sorts of things that can cause injury.

Grasses. The first are grasses that cut the snout and poke the eyes. The worst is foxtail, a sharp seed that, left untreated, can burrow into the skin and cause infections. Make sure you watch your dog for signs of grass seeds, like vigorous head shaking, pawing at the snout, or constant sneezing. Remove any seeds you find with your fingers or with tweezers.

Scrapes and cuts. Scrapes, cuts, and punctures happen. If not serious, wash the cut with water and apply a Betadine solution. Don't close a puncture wound, as this could cause more serious infection. It's better to keep a puncture wound open, covered with a gauze square, until you can get to your vet.

Pad injuries. Pad injuries can be common if you haven't taken your dog out much. The pads can get abraded, cut, or blistered. It's best to clean them up with a Betadine solution and then to apply an antibiotic cream. I carry a tube of superglue, which can be applied to the pads to form a shield.

Water danger and CPR. Even the most water-loving dog can get in trouble and—without proper supervision—can drown. Creeks can be swift, waterfall pools deep, and most high-mountain lakes are ringed with rocks, making it difficult for a struggling animal to escape.

If your dog has taken in a lot of water and is struggling to breathe, pick him up by his hind legs so he hangs upside down, then have someone close the dog's mouth and blow into his nose several times to dispel the water and to get air to his lungs.

If your dog isn't breathing, begin CPR immediately. Lay your dog on his right side and check his pulse by placing your fingertips on the left side of his chest behind his elbow. If there's no pulse, clear your dog's airway, close his mouth, and blow into his nose until his lungs expand. Then push on his chest four times, depressing 1 to 2 inches. Repeat these steps about fifteen times per minute, until your dog regains consciousness, or for five minutes.

Soreness. Sore muscles can hit your dog as easily as they hit you. If, after a hard day of hiking, your dog is limping or lethargic—and you can't find an injury—it may be sore muscles. Your vet can prescribe a small amount of anti-inflammatory medication, but simple buffered aspirin works really well. Stay away from uncoated aspirin, since it tends to dissolve in the stomach and can cause some ailments. Buffered aspirin is designed to dissolve in the intestine, which won't cause any stomach issues.

With most anything, it pays to be observant. Watch how your dog is reacting, and check your pet often for injury. Look inside her ears, mouth, and between her toes for foreign objects or cuts.

And remember that even the friendliest, most loving pooch can snap when she is scared or in pain, so always apply a muzzle before treating a wound or injury.

What Goes in a Doggy First-Aid Kit?

Having a canine first-aid kit is essential, even if it has only the barebones. For a comprehensive kit, though, carry the following items when heading into the wild with a canine companion:

Instruments
- Scissors/bandage scissors
- Toenail clippers
- Rectal thermometer (a healthy dog's temperature be should 101 when taken rectally)

Cleansers and disinfectants
- 3% hydrogen peroxide
- Betadine
- Canine eyewash (available at any large pet-supply store).

Topical antibiotics and ointments (nonprescription)
- Calamine lotion
- Triple antibiotic ointment (bacitracin, neomycin, or polymyxin)
- Baking soda (for bee stings)
- Vaseline
- Stop-bleeding powder

Medications (nonprescription)
- Enteric-coated aspirin or Bufferin
- Imodium A-D
- Pepto-Bismol

Dressings and bandages
- Gauze pads (4 inches square)
- Gauze roll
- Nonstick pads
- Adhesive tape (1-inch and 2-inch rolls)

Miscellaneous
- Muzzle
- Dog booties
- Any prescription medication your dog needs

For Extended Trips
Consult your vet about additional prescription medications or other supplies that might be needed in an emergency situation, including:
- Oral antibiotics

- Eye medications
- Ear medications
- Emetics (to induce vomiting)
- Pain medications and anti-inflammatories
- Suturing materials for large open wounds

Hydration

When hiking, you and your pet should be dogged about staying hydrated. In semiarid conditions, pack more water than you'll possibly need. A good rule to follow is 8 ounces of water for yourself—and for your dog—every 15 minutes, or about a liter an hour. Seems like a lot, doesn't it? Well, just a 2 percent loss of fluids in a 150-pound person equals 3 pounds, according to the good folks at Camelbak, makers of hydration systems; and that means a loss of energy. It's worse for your dog, since he will literally play until dropping.

Dehydration can set in quickly, which can lead to heat exhaustion and heatstroke, for both you and your dog.

Learn to identify heat exhaustion and heatstroke in your dog. If your dog starts to pant excessively and the insides of her ears are bright red, these are warning signs to stop and have a drink (or a swim, if there's a water source nearby). If your dog exhibits weakness, staggers, or faints, these are the signs of heatstroke, a very serious condition that requires immediate attention: it's imperative to douse your dog with cool water or to let her sit in a lake or mountain stream.

When hiking, I tend not to treat the water my dogs drink. Giardia, a protozoal parasite, is common in all

Hydration is not just for you, as rambunctious dogs can get dehydrated too. Make sure to stop at water areas often.

akes and streams in the West. It attacks the host's intestinal track and can ead to weight loss, vomiting, diarrhea, and lack of appetite. While nasty n humans, giardia tends not to infect dogs as often. Estimates in some egions say that 70 percent of the dog population has giardia present in heir systems, but the dogs don't get the symptoms. If you have any concerns, by all means, treat your dog's water with a good filter. Nowadays, ilters that screen out giardia and other nasties can be purchased for less han $50.

Pack with Care

When planning a backcountry adventure, or just a simple day hike, be prepared. Bring the right gear and bring plenty of it, for you and your dog.

For the backcountry, I don't pack a stitch of cotton clothing, relying instead on synthetic fabrics that wick moisture away from my body and that help me stay warm, even in a downpour. To this I add lightweight raingear and plenty of synthetic socks. Dry—and clean—socks are golden on the trail.

So are a broad-brimmed hat and stocking cap. The brimmed hat is there to keep the sun from beating you down; the stocking cap is useful for evening use, since you lose most of your body heat through your noggin.

You shouldn't neglect your dog's comfort. If going on an overnight trip, you'll need to bring a blanket or thermal pad for your dog to sleep on, since dogs can lose body heat to the ground just as easily as humans can. Large trash bags can be fashioned into cheap raingear, for both you and your dog, in a pinch.

The Mountaineers Ten Essentials: A Systems Approach

1. Navigation (map and compass)
2. Sun protection (sunglasses and sunscreen)
3. Insulation (extra clothing)
4. Illumination (headlamp or flashlight)
5. First-aid supplies
6. Fire (firestarter and matches/lighter)
7. Repair kit and tools (including knife)
8. Nutrition (extra food)
9. Hydration (extra water)
10. Emergency shelter

The Mountaineers Ten Essentials are a must (see sidebar), but here are the slightly modified ten essentials I bring for myself:

1. **Extra clothing.** This means more clothing than you expect to wear; always plan for the worst weather. If you get injured or lost, you won't be moving around to generate heat, so be prepared. And always layer. It's much easier to take off clothing than it is to put on what you don't have.

2. **Extra food.** If you've got leftovers after an uneventful trip, you've planned well. But if you get lost or injured, that extra food can make the difference between comfort and disaster. Good choices include ramen noodles, oatmeal, and trail mix. Each is minimal in weight but packs a punch in carbohydrates and fat.

3. **Water filter.** I can't stress enough the need to stay hydrated. Carrying a water filter means you can "tank up" on water, whether from a mountain stream or lake.

4. **Knife or multipurpose tool.** A one-thousand-and-one uses item: for everything from whittling kindling for a warming fire to first-aid applications and gutting a fish to fixing a pack or pair of boots with handy pliers.

5. **First-aid kit.** First, take an American Red Cross or Boy Scout first-aid training class. Then be sure to pack a first-aid kit on every outing. By all means, share some of the components of your doggie first-aid kit.

6. **Map and compass.** Take a course in map and compass reading. Then take a U.S. Geological Survey (USGS) map of the area you plan to visit and a quality compass. I know a lot of people are switching to Global Positioning System units, since many have come down in price to under $100. But a compass doesn't run off batteries that can fail—and I think it's important to pass on the unappreciated skill of navigation by map and compass.

7. **Emergency firestarter and matches.** Normally, I carry both a Zippo lighter (always remembering to refill before a trip) and matches in a waterproof container. Nothing beats a warming fire on a cold evening, not just for comfort, but for the calming effect it has on people (and on dogs, of course). Candles and firestarter tape are good options for lighting wet wood, and a battery and steel wool (touch the wool to both ends of the battery) makes a fast, ferocious light. Just be sure to carry

Being prepared on the trail, even if it is in an urban area, is key to having a good hike with your dog.

the steel wool and battery in separate, waterproof containers.

8. **Sunglasses.** I can't live without a good pair of sunglasses. I also have polarized lenses, so I can see the fish I'm trying to catch.

9. **Duct tape.** You can repair just about anything—including using it to close a wound—with duct tape. I wrap extra tape around a plastic water bottle to use as needed.

10. **Fishing rod, tackle.** I love to fish, just for the pure recreation of it. But in a pinch, I can feed myself if I'm stuck in the backcountry for an extra day.

Those are your essentials. You should also have the Ten Canine Essentials for your dog:

1. **Obedience training.** Before you set foot on a trail, make sure your dog is trained and can be trusted to behave when faced with other hikers, other dogs, wildlife, and an assortment of strange scents and sights in the backcountry.

2. **Doggie backpack.** Lets the dog carry his own gear.

3. **First-aid kit.** (see page 30, What Goes in a Doggy First-Aid Kit?)

4. **Dog food and trail treats.** You should bring more food than your dog normally consumes since he will be burning more calories than normal, and if you do end up having to spend

an extra night out there, you need to keep the pup fed, too. Trail treats serve the same purpose for the dog as they do for you—quick energy and a pick-me-up during a strenuous day of hiking.

5. **Water and water bowl.** Don't count on there being water along the trail for your dog. Pack enough extra water to meet all your dog's drinking needs.

6. **Leash and collar, or harness.** Even if your dog is absolutely trained to voice commands and stays at heel without a leash, sometimes leashes are required by law or just by common courtesy, so you should have one handy at all times.

7. **Insect repellent.** Be aware that some animals, and some people, have strong negative reactions to DEET-based repellents. So, before leaving home, dab a little DEET-based repellent on a patch of your dog's fur to see if he reacts to it. Look for signs of drowsiness, lethargy, and/or nausea. Restrict repellent applications to those places your dog can't lick—the back of the neck and around the ears (staying well clear of the eyes and inner ears) are where mosquitoes will be looking for exposed skin to bite.

8. **ID tags and picture identification.** Your dog should always wear ID tags, and I'd heartily recommend microchipping your dog as well. To do this, a vet injects a tiny encoded microchip under the skin between your dog's shoulders. If your dog ever gets lost and is picked up by animal control, or is taken to a vet's office, a quick pass over the dog's back with a hand scanner will reveal the chip and allow for quick identification. Microchipping is so prevalent that virtually every vet and animal shelter automatically scans every unknown dog they come in contact with to check for chips. The picture identification should go in your pack. If your dog gets lost, you can use the picture to make flyers and handbills to post in the surrounding communities.

9. **Dog booties.** These can be used to protect your dog's feet from rough ground or harsh vegetation. They are also great at keeping bandages secure if your dog damages his pads.

10. **Compact roll of plastic bags and trowel.** You'll need the bags to clean up after your dog on popular trails. When conditions warrant, you can use the trowel to take care of your dog's

waste. Dig a small hole several inches deep in the forest duff, deposit the dog waste, and fill in the hole.

Obstacles, Wild Animals, and Weather

Being outdoors on a new trail can lead to sensory overload for your dog. Even the most well-mannered pooch can become a handful. It's just one of many obstacles awaiting hikers and their furry friends. But with preparation you can certainly cut the odds so that the following won't be an issue.

Poison Oak

Poison oak is the itch that keeps on giving, especially if you hike with dogs. The oil that causes the itch, urushiol, can crystallize and linger in pet fur for weeks—and can continue to infect you every time you pet your pooch (your dog can also transfer the oils to pet beds and couch fabrics, as I discovered in my bachelor days).

In Northern California, poison oak is abundant on trails below 4000 feet (the plant doesn't grow above that elevation). Most people subscribe to the "leaves of three, let it be" motto; however, most dogs don't and go charging off into the shrub with abandon.

Poison oak grows as a deciduous shrub up to 30 inches high. It has triple leaves that are similar in shape to oak leaves and have smooth hair underneath. The plant is dark green, but the leaves can be bright red. The berries start out white, but turn brown.

As a general rule, if you don't get the urushiol off your skin within 30 minutes of contact, you're likely to bust out in a nasty rash. You can carry over-the-counter soaps and lotions for yourself, but just make sure of one thing before heading back to your car—if you suspect that your dogs have romped through poison oak, rinse them off in a stream or lake. Then bathe them with a good dog shampoo when you get home.

And wouldn't you know it? Dogs are immune to the itch.

Poison oak is the bane of hikers on trails under 4000 feet in elevation. The oil the plant gives off can get into a dog's fur and infect you weeks after contact.

Mosquitoes and Ticks

These two pests are the bane of both man and beast. While mosquito and tick bites will both leave welts and scratchy spots, each bite can carry much more.

Mosquitoes. There are more than two hundred different species of mosquito in the United States, and the insect is the most common carrier, or vector, of disease in the world. Bites can cause severe reactions in dogs, but the most pressing problem today is the threat of the West Nile virus.

The virus was first reported in Uganda in 1937 and has spread rapidly to all temperate regions of the world. Indeed, as of this writing, in the United States only four states—Oregon, Nevada, Utah, and Arizona—have yet to report a single case. Since 1999, there has been one reported case of a dog that died from the disease, according to the Centers for Disease Control and Prevention.

Still, prevention for both you and your pet are paramount in the backcountry. Most people infected by the West Nile Virus show no symptoms. About 20 percent develop flulike symptoms, and in some cases the infection can lead to encephalitis or meningitis.

Worse than West Nile for dogs, thirty species of mosquito carry heartworm larvae. This is a deadly problem in dogs. One bite from a carrier mosquito can deliver millions of microfilaria, or young, worms that travel through the bloodstream and clog the heart.

It's best to pack insect repellent containing DEET. Just another reminder, apply a little to your dog's fur to make sure she doesn't have a reaction, and always avoid getting it near your pet's eyes.

Ticks. Ick. These little pests can carry Lyme disease, Rocky Mountain spotted fever, and a few other potentially fatal diseases. Some diseases and symptoms to watch out for in dogs include:

- Babesiosis: lethargy, weakness, pale gums, appetite loss
- Ehrlichiosis: muscle aches, high fever (most dogs have a core body temperature of 101 to 102 degrees)
- Lyme disease: swollen joints, fever, poor appetite, vomiting (some dogs will show no symptoms)
- Tick paralysis: odd gait from uncoordinated back legs, unsteadiness, gradual paralysis

Ticks also are a chore to remove, once you or your dog is bitten. Ticks range in size from a sesame seed to a fingernail, once gorged with blood.

If you take your dog on hikes regularly, you should check him daily. If you find a tick attached, use a fine-pointed pair of tweezers and grasp he tick at the head, but don't squeeze. Use a slow and steady motion and pull the tick's head straight out from the skin, then clean the wound with soap and water.

There are all sorts of topical and chewable products available from your veterinarian to combat these tiny pests. Find out which products might be right for your pet, and use them.

Bears and Mountain Lions

It's estimated that there are between 15,000 and 22,000 American black bear in California. Mountain lion populations are harder to track, since little is known about the cougar's comeback in the state (they are federally protected). Current estimates, derived from hunters and road kills, range from 10,000 to 50,000 across the United States and 4000 to 6000 in California alone.

Bears. Cases of bear attacks on humans are rare; however, there were two reported attacks in 2003, according to the California Department of

Trinity takes a look at Castle Lake near the town of Mount Shasta.

Fish and Game (DFG). Black bears tend to shy away from human and dog contact and will generally flee if they spot you in time. With that said, bears are the Mr. Magoo of the forest. They have poor eyesight. What they can do is smell—extraordinarily well—and hear.

Dogs can be a blessing and a curse when it comes to bears. A leashed dog, or one that is under strict voice command, can alert you to the presence of a bear. A dog running loose, however, may give chase, which may cause a bear to turn and defend itself. In writing this book, I've seen more bears in six months than in the previous eight years of living in Northern California. Go figure. Each encounter ended as soon as it started, by following these guidelines:

- Hike with a group and during daylight hours (bears are more active in the evening and early morning).
- Keep your dog on a leash.
- Be aware of your surroundings and watch for bear signs. Footprints, claw marks on trees, and scat are all signs that a bear has passed your way.
- Talk or sing while on the trail. If bears can hear you coming they'll likely hightail it the other way.
- Leave the hair spray, cologne, hand creams, scented soaps, and other stinky products at home. Use unscented products, and avoid anything that makes you smell like a huge, tasty treat.

If you're camping overnight in the backcountry, make sure you know the proper way to hang or store food while in camp. Sloppy backpackers make for educated—and bothersome—bears. Some general guidelines include:

- Never clean fish within 100 feet of camp.
- Store all food, including dog food, in designated stuff sacks; hang them overnight and when you leave camp for a day hike. Suspend food bags at least 12 feet off the ground and 8-10 feet from the nearest tree trunk, or use a bear-proof canister to store food. A great website for learning how to hang food is available from the National Park Service at *www.nps.gov/seki/bearhang.htm*.
- Don't eat, or feed your dog, in your tent. Spilled food or food odors will permeate the tent fabric and serve as a beacon to a bear's nose.

Mountain lions. Chances are, you'll never see a mountain lion in the wild. In eight years, I've been lucky to catch a streak of gold twice—and I still can't be sure if it was a cougar. However, they will see you. These

Scully takes a breather on a cool granite rock.

are solitary hunters that normally prey on big game, like deer, bighorn sheep, and elk.

Generally, mountain lions are calm, quiet, and elusive. They are most commonly found in areas with plentiful prey and adequate cover. Such conditions exist in mountain subdivisions, urban fringes, and open spaces. Consequently, the number of mountain lion/human interactions has increased.

Surprisingly, there has been little research done on how to avoid an attack by a mountain lion. The following suggestions, provided by the DFG, are based on studies of leopard, tiger, and lastly, mountain lion attacks:

- Don't hike alone: go in groups, with adults supervising children.
- Keep children and dogs close to you: observations of captured wild mountain lions reveal that the animals seem especially drawn to children. Keep children within your sight at all times.
- Don't approach a lion: most mountain lions will try to avoid a confrontation. Give them a way to escape.
- Don't run from a lion: running may stimulate a mountain lion's instinct to chase. Instead, stand and face the animal. Make eye contact. If you have small children with you, pick them up if possible so they don't panic and run. Although it may be awkward, pick them up without bending over or turning away from the mountain lion.
- Don't crouch or bend over: in Nepal, a researcher studying tigers

and leopards watched the big cats kill cattle and domestic water buffalo while ignoring humans standing nearby. He surmised that a human standing up is just not the right shape for a cat's prey. On the other hand, a person squatting or bending over looks a lot like a four-legged animal. If you're in mountain lion country, avoid squatting, crouching, or bending over.

- Do all you can to appear larger: raise your arms; open your jacket if you're wearing one. Again, pick up small children. Throw stones, branches, or whatever you can reach without crouching or turning your back. Wave your arms slowly and speak firmly in a loud voice. The idea is to convince the mountain lion that you're not prey and that you may be a danger to it.

- Fight back if attacked: a hiker in Southern California used a rock to fend off a mountain lion that was attacking his son. Others have fought back successfully with sticks, caps, jackets, garden tools, and their bare hands. Since a mountain lion usually tries to bite the head or neck, try to remain standing and face the attacking animal.

Weather

Yes, everyone talks about it, people try to forecast it, but let's face it, weather just might be the biggest threat to man and beast in the backcountry. Northern California weather is notoriously finicky, and mountain weather can change in a matter of minutes.

In the summer months, thunderstorms can come up quickly and produce heavy rains and, more importantly, lightning. A sudden rain squall can drop temperatures 15 to 20 degrees in minutes. Remember always to pack raingear and to dress in layers (please, please, please avoid cotton) to avoid hypothermia or a cooling of the body's core temperature.

According to the National Oceanic and Atmospheric Administration (NOAA), lightning originates at 15,000 to 25,000 feet above sea level as raindrops are swept upward and turn to ice. Most cloud-to-cloud lightning takes place in this region of ice and water. The charges then move down as if on steps and eventually encounter something on the ground— like a tall tree, or metal tower—that provides a good connection. Here are some guidelines for lightning safety:

- Lightning can strike as much as 10 miles away from the rain area of a thunderstorm. If you can hear thunder, you're within striking distance. Seek shelter immediately. Use the 30-6 rule: When you see lightning, count the time until you hear thunder. If that time is 30 seconds or less, the thunderstorm is within 6 miles of you and is dangerous.

- Be the lowest point. Lightning hits the tallest object. In the mountains if you are above tree line, you are the highest object around. Quickly get below tree line and get into a grove of small trees. Don't be the second tallest object during a lightning storm! Crouch down if you are in an exposed area.

California poppy, the state flower, is a constant sight during spring and summer hikes in Northern California.

- If you can't get to a shelter, stay away from trees. Crouch in the open, keeping twice as far away from a tree as it is tall.
- Get out of the water. It's a great conductor of electricity. Stay off the beach and out of small boats or canoes. Don't stand in puddles of water, even if you're wearing rubber boots.
- Avoid metal! Drop metal-framed backpacks, stay away from clotheslines, fences, exposed sheds, and electrically conductive elevated objects.
- Move away from other people, several yards away. Don't huddle in a group.

Expect that Mother Nature will try to throw you a curve each and every time you venture outdoors. Come prepared, pack your raingear, and make sure to call ahead and get the latest forecast for the area you plan to visit. People also can use a NOAA weather radio (a radio set to tune in one of the national weather frequencies), which costs between $30 and $75.

How to Use This Book

Trail guides are hardly an exact science. What was true of a trail last summer might not be the case next summer. No guide can provide all the details of a trail or stay current with constantly changing conditions and administrative rules. Before heading out on any adventure, it's best to call ahead to the land management agency to get the latest trail report—and make sure the trail is open to you and your dog.

With each hike in this guide, you'll find round-trip or one-way mileage, hiking time, high point, elevation gain, best times to hike, water availability, USGS or other mapping resources, contact information, and directions to the trailhead and a trail description.

Round-trip or one-way miles and hiking time. I can hike a mile in about 20 minutes, which is the estimate I used in determining time and distance in this guide. I also tried to factor in time for steep grades and rough tread. You might find that my estimates are too low, or too high. They are merely tools to help you plan a trip.

Elevation gain. The elevation gain is the total feet in elevation gained from the trailhead to the end of the hike. Thus, elevation gain combined with distance will give you a good indication of the overall difficulty of a hike.

Best hiking time. As for the best hiking time, this too is a subjective tool meant as a guide, not as an absolute. I like to hike some trails in spring, when there's still snow on the ground. My wife prefers not to be cold—in any instance. Many high-mountain trails might not be passable until July. It's best to use the contact information to get the latest trail report.

Many of the trails—and I always indicate which—can be hiked year-round, with or without snowshoes. If you've never tried a snowshoe hike, I urge you to try it. Winter can be an absolutely fantastic time to revisit a trail you know by heart in the summer.

Maps. While some USGS maps haven't been updated since the 1970s, I believe USGS maps are still the best to carry. I use the 7.5-minute series, which are available nearly everywhere, including online at *http://ngmdb.usgs.gov/* or at *www.topozone.com.*

How the Trails Were Selected

With nineteen national forests comprising 20 million acres in California, the chance to explore is nearly overwhelming. Factor in BLM lands, regional parks, and state lands, and you'd have a book that could go on forever.

This book isn't meant to be a complete resource for all the trails in Northern California, nor is it a guide to the best of them. My goal was to present a sampling of what is available, from the wilds of far Northern California to the easy day hikes of the Bay Area's regional park and

Some hikes in this book were selected based on seasonal wildflower blooms.

preserve system. I sought to include day hikes and overnighters. I tried to stay away from those trails that are used heavily, since some people just don't like sharing the trail with dogs.

I tried for a sampling of trails that would appeal to humans and dogs. Water features, places with awe-inspiring views, and simple places where a dog might run free are high on my list of "musts."

I avoided steep, rocky places where possible, and most waterfalls. I tried to find places where the reward is a pond, lake, or a gentle stream—I've yet to meet a dog that didn't love to swim.

Some of the trails were selected for their gentleness, to get those newbies with dogs out and about. I've tried to list a few trails that will appeal to summer hikers and that can double as snowshoe hikes in the winter.

With all this in mind, I came up with seventy-five hikes from my experiences with Scully and Trinity on trails centered around Redding, Sacramento, and the San Francisco Bay Area. Certainly, enjoy them all—but don't limit yourself to just these seventy-five. Find what works for you and continue to expand you and your dog's appreciation for the wonderful wilds of Northern California.

Keep Our Open Spaces Open: Get Involved

I wrote this book in hopes of sharing my love of the outdoors with other dog owners. Trinity, Scully, and I have traveled far and wide in search of adventure, enjoying a simple day hike along a mountain stream as well as all-out backpacking treks into some of California's more rugged public lands.

The trails exist for our enjoyment, and for the enjoyment of future generations. Use the trails often, but always remember to protect them as well. Be careful with your actions, so no one can complain that dogs cause damage to our trails.

Also, be aware of what is happening to our public lands. Stay informed and stay involved. It might be as simple as writing your representative urging them to support wilderness protection, or even asking them to allow dogs in new regional parks and open spaces. For more information on open space issues, contact the following groups:

California Wilderness Coalition
2655 Portage Bay East, Suite 5
Davis, CA 95616
Phone: (530) 758-0380
Fax: (530) 758-0382
info@calwild.org
www.calwild.org

Peninsula Access for Dogs (PADS)
1165 Eureka Avenue
Los Altos, CA 94024
Fax: (650) 851-9341
pads7@prusik.com
http://prusik.com/pads

The Mountaineers
300 Third Avenue West
Seattle, WA 98119
(206) 284-6310
www.mountaineers.org

A Note About Safety

Safety is an important concern in all outdoor activities. No guidebook can alert you to every hazard or anticipate the limitations of every reader.

Therefore, the descriptions of roads, trails, routes, and natural features in this book are not representations that a particular place or excursion will be safe for your party. When you follow any of the routes described in this book, you assume responsibility for your own safety. Under normal conditions, such excursions require the usual attention to traffic, road and trail conditions, weather, terrain, the capabilities of your party, and other factors. Keeping informed on current conditions and exercising common sense are the keys to a safe, enjoyable outing.

The Mountaineers Books

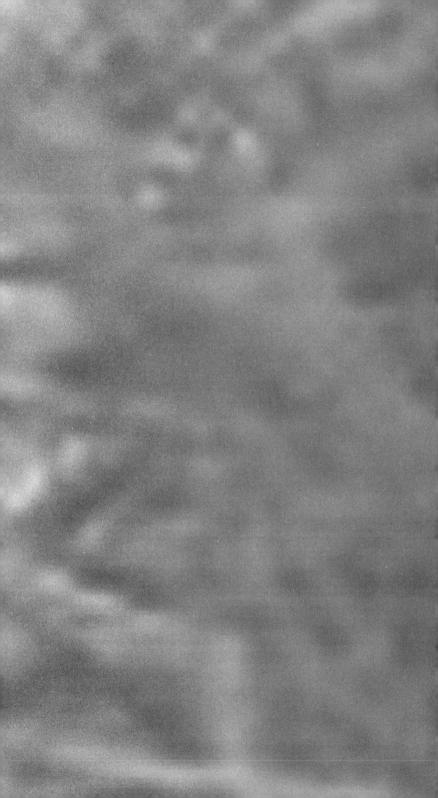

PART 2

The Trails

SHASTA-CASCADE

1. PCT to Seven Lakes Basin

Round trip: 6 miles
Hiking time: 5 hours or overnight
High point: 6900 feet
Elevation gain: 1250 feet
Best hiking time: Early June through late October
Water: Only from Seven Lakes Basin lakes; bring your own for the approach hike
Maps: USGS Mumbo Basin, USGS Seven Lakes Basin
Contact: Shasta-Trinity National Forest, Mount Shasta Ranger District, (530) 926-4511

Getting there: Take the Central Mount Shasta exit off Interstate 5 and turn left. Follow this road west and south on South Old Stage Road and W. A. Barr Road. Follow it in an arc around Lake Siskiyou and you'll notice the road changes to Forest Road 26. Follow this paved, scenic road 18.3 miles to Gumboot Saddle (there's a signed parking area on the right), which is 2.5 miles past Gumboot Lake and its free campground.

The drive in to this trailhead alone is enough to lower your heart rate, as well as your stress level. Get on the trail, and you'll soon realize that this trek requires little effort—but the rewards are fantastic.

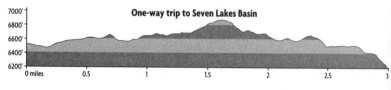

Seven Lakes Basin sits like a jewel beneath the Pacific Crest Trail.

While trekking along the wide Pacific Crest Trail, you can't help but stop often to take in the 360 degrees of panoramic pleasure. From various points, you'll glimpse 14,162-foot Mount Shasta, the granitic splendor of Castle Crags, the volcanic magnificence of Gray Rocks, the Trinity Divide, the Trinity Alps, and the best of the Klamath Mountains. Add to that a couple of dandy lakes where swimming and fishing are king, and you've got the makings of the quintessential weekend getaway.

The trail into the basin begins across the road from the parking area. Look for a wide path and the PCT marker that indicates trail uses. After several minutes of forested walking, you'll burst forth into an opening, where several rocky clearings give an unimpeded view of the mountains and forests of this heavily glaciated and volcanic area. In spring, the path will be flecked with wildflowers, notably yellow sulfur flowers, sweet pea, and blue lupine.

You'll get to a PCT thru-hiker campsite off to the left of the trail in just 0.3 mile. It's here that you'll get your first look at a towering Mount Shasta, and depending on the time of year, it'll be cloaked in white or wearing the browns and grays of summer. Soon, Mount Eddy, the head-waters of the Sacramento River, and Gumboot Lake come into view. Look west for great views of Mumbo Lake (great for trout) and the forested Mumbo Basin.

The trail enters a keyhole in the mountain and there's a trail fork at

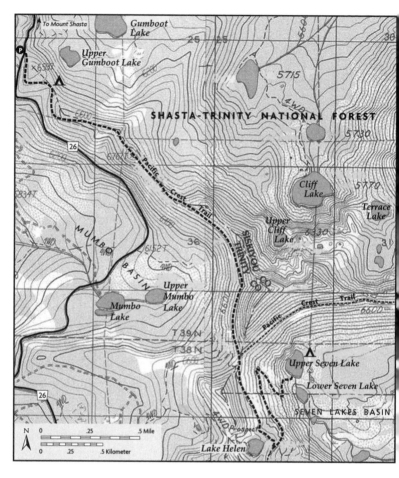

the saddle, about 2.5 miles in. From this vantage point, you'll be able to spot Boulder Mountain rising above the basin's largest lake, Echo (it's privately owned, the owner is notoriously cranky and it's best left unexplored). You'll also get views of Lassen Peak, Magee Peak, and Burney Mountain to the southeast.

To quickly make the descent into Seven Lakes Basin, go 30 more feet on the PCT and look for a faint and unmarked trail that dips down to the right. It will soon intersect an old four-wheel-drive path that you can follow right to Upper Seven Lake, about a 0.5-mile distance. Upper Seven Lake is ringed with rocks and vegetation, but its north shore has a dandy beach that just begs you to take a dip. The lake has a healthy population of brook and rainbow trout, which will rise to a fly or copper-colored ure (I never leave home without a 0.25-ounce copper Kastmaster).

The best campsites are the farthest east of two spots that are too close to the water's edge; Lower Seven Lake is 100 yards to the south. It's shallow, muddy, and has no campsites.

Trails snake their way throughout the basin, which allows for some great exploration of this area. This hike is a good primer for families who want to get into the backpacking lifestyle.

2. Castle and Heart Lakes

Round trip: 3.4 miles
Hiking time: 3 hours
High point: 6000 feet
Elevation gain: 700 feet
Best hiking time: Mid-May through late October; snowshoe the rest of the year
Water: From Castle Lake
Maps: USGS Seven Lakes Basin, USGS Dunsmuir, USFS Castle Crags Wilderness
Contact: Shasta-Trinity National Forest, Mount Shasta Ranger District, (530) 926-4511

Getting there: Leave Interstate 5 at the Central Mount Shasta exit and turn left at the stop sign. Travel west and south on South Old Stage Road and W. A. Barr Road. Cross the Box Canyon Dam, which forms Lake Siskiyou from the upper Sacramento River, and turn left at the signed Castle Lake Road. Follow it 7.1 miles to the paved parking lot (the road is plowed throughout the winter). The trail crosses Castle Lake's outlet stream to the east.

Since 1968, students from the University of California at Davis have been studying Castle Lake in the area of limnology, from the Greek word *limne*, which means marsh or lake.

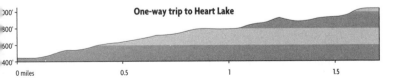

One-way trip to Heart Lake

The science helps researchers understand some things about the world's freshwater: how healthy it is, what's happening to it, and how water quality can improve with time—and interference by people. What the budding researchers have found is that despite heavy year-round use, Castle Lake continues to be one of the most unspoiled subalpine lakes in the world. Start at Castle Lake and take this trip up to tiny Heart Lake and you'll have a great appreciation of these north state gems.

This trek in fall offers up many fewer people, and you'll be able to see the gradual color change, from greens to golds and browns. In the winter months, you'll still be able to pick your way through the forest and up the ridge, but if the snow is too deep, you can satisfy your exploration needs by following the western shoreline of Castle Lake.

At its start, the trail immediately begins its ascent toward Mount Bradley.

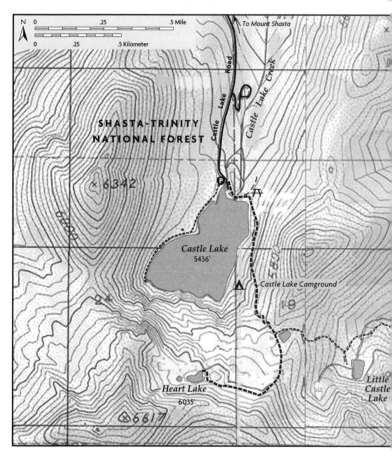

Castle Lake, where dog smells abound, is one of the most pristine subalpine lakes in the world.

Ridge and tiny Heart Lake just below. This steep and rocky path soon bursts from the canopy of alder, oak, and pine and affords the first overall glimpses of the glaciated Castle Lake basin. You'll reach the saddle in little more than 0.5 mile; keep looking for an unmarked trail to the right that leads to a seasonal marsh. Follow this path through the upper meadows (erupting with wildflowers in the spring) another 0.5 mile to Heart Lake.

Let the dogs take a dip, soak your own dogs, and don't forget to hike over to a rocky ledge for a breathtaking view of Castle Lake and Mount Shasta to the north. Side trips include a trek up to Mount Bradley Ridge or a short downhill hike to Little Castle Lake, where there's an inviting summer campsite.

To extend your stay in this outdoor playground, visit the Forest Service's Castle Lake Campground, about 0.5 mile south of the Castle Lake parking lot. This free campsite has portable toilets (there also are toilets at the parking lot), but no drinking water. But with one of the world's most unspoiled lakes just ahead, drink up (purify first) the cool, clean waters of Castle Lake.

3. Squaw Valley Creek Trail

Round trip: 10 miles
Hiking time: 6 hours or overnight
High point: 2800 feet
Elevation gain: 200 feet
Best hiking time: March through November
Water: From Squaw Valley Creek
Maps: Free from the Shasta-Trinity National Forest, or USGS Girard
   Ridge
Contact: Shasta-Trinity National Forest, McCloud Ranger District,
   (530) 964-2184

Getting there: Turn right at the McCloud central business district and follow the signs for Squaw Valley Creek Road and the McCloud Reservoir. Continue on this road for 6.1 miles. Just past an RV and camp park named "Friday's Retreat," turn right onto Squaw Valley Creek Road. The sign says "rough road," but this dirt path can be handled easily in the family sedan. Continue on this road for 3.1 miles, where you'll cross over a concrete bridge. The parking area, trailhead, and restroom will be on your immediate left once you cross the bridge.

Simplicity is the basis of greatness, and people who take the time to discover this hike will find something new to cherish each and every time out.

Over time, Squaw Valley Creek has sliced the surrounding dark basalt rock into a cascade of cool pools that babble under a canopy of mature, mixed conifer forest that includes Pacific yew, incense cedar, and Douglas fir. The undercanopy includes black oak, willow, dogwood, alder, and vine maple, with wild ginger, iris, and wild rose clinging to the mossy ground. Indian rhubarb grows thick at the water's rocky edge, hiding delightful pools where man and beast can soak on hot summer days.

Given the elevation, poison oak also does very well here. Be sure to wash your dogs before loading them back in your car, and be sure to give

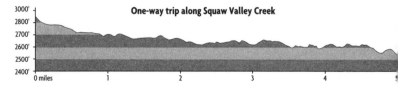

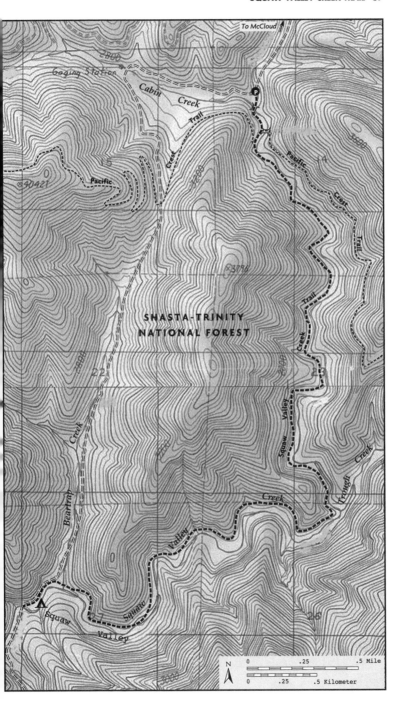

A wooden bridge crosses Squaw Valley Creek and connects the Squaw Valley Creek Trail with the Pacific Crest Trail.

them a good bath when you get home. The volatile oil that causes your skin to itch—urushiol—sticks to dog fur and can cause a breakout days later.

Every season brings a new reason to visit this trail, which offers a lot of level ground and a few gentle climbs. Spring, when the dogwoods are in bloom, brings anglers to the creek, where native rainbow trout will rise to suck down a meal of hatching aquatic bugs. Summer is the time for birders, swimmers, and wildlife watchers. Be sure to pack the binoculars for the chance to view mountain quail, common nighthawk, hairy woodpecker, Pacific-slope flycatchers, Swainson's thrush, cedar waxwing, evening grosbeak, and a host of other species. If you're quiet, there's always a chance to glimpse a black-tailed deer munching on vegetation or a black bear sipping from the creek. Fall brings on a burst of color from the undercanopy. The creek, which rarely dips from view along the trail, flows through a blaze of orange, crimson, and yellow.

A sturdy wooden bridge takes hikers across Cabin Creek, then the trail hugs the west side of Squaw Valley Creek for the duration of the trek. The Forest Service has completed 5 miles of trail and is in the process of adding more miles to the experience. The complete out-and-back trek can be leisurely done in 6 hours, leaving plenty of time to play in the chilly water. Be sure to bring a water filter to drink from this spring-fed creek.

At Cabin Creek, the 2650-mile Pacific Crest Trail crosses Squaw Valley Creek. During the summer months, there's always the possibility of talking with thru-hikers about their adventures.

While the chance to take a dip along this stream is constant, a not-to-be-missed pool is located at 2.2 miles. A wide, smooth section of basalt makes for a great place to catch some sun and have a picnic. Soft sand coats the bottom of this pool, big enough and deep enough for several people—and their dogs.

The dense undercanopy slowly begins to swallow the trail at 4 miles. Along a rocky wall, the trail finally gives over to a thicket of alder and it's time to turn around.

This hike also can be turned into an overnight trip, with good campsites near the south terminus of the trail. Camp at least 200 feet from the creek and be sure to follow Leave No Trace ethics.

4. McCloud Waterfalls

Round trip: 3.2 miles
Hiking time: 2 hours
High point: 3600 feet
Elevation gain: 200 feet
Best hiking time: Year-round; snowshoe in winter, falls more powerful in spring
Water: From Fowlers Campground; or from the river
Map: USGS Lake McCloud
Contact: Shasta-Trinity National Forest, McCloud Ranger District, (530) 926-2184

Getting there: Take the Highway 89 exit from Interstate 5 and drive 15 miles to the Fowlers Campground. Go about 0.5 mile, stay straight at a road fork, bear right in another 50 yards, and then continue another 0.5 mile to the trailhead and the Lower Falls of the McCloud Picnic Area.

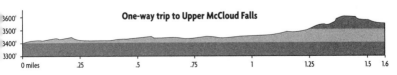

Middle McCloud Falls, mid-spring (photo by Marc Soares)

To tune in to a wild river boasting three fantastic waterfalls on a hike that's a piece of cake seems too good to be true, but that's what you get with this trek. This trio of exhilarating falls are all granite-ringed, and that's where the similarities end. The Lower Falls are by far the tamest. The Middle Falls radiate a spiritual feel; a soul can easily bring back the days when the Wintu Indians must have found deep peace on one of the big rocks at the scene. The Upper Falls aren't as photogenic as the Middle Falls, but are perhaps the most unique looking, and certainly carry the most water force.

You get a lot for a little energy expense, unless you make it a much longer hike or even a backpack trip by continuing on a new trail section (built in the late 1990s) along the banks of the fast-flowing McCloud River. After 14 miles, you come out of a very remote river region into the tiny community of Algoma. There are no fees for the hike and no permit required unless you intend to stay the night along the river.

Start at the Lower Falls. Up to 40 feet wide in late spring, these falls spill 15 vertical feet into a foamy avalanche of white froth, then into a 25-yard-long pool. Picnickers and anglers relax along the granite slab field overlooking the inspirational scene.

Continue along the river; Fowlers Campground borders this narrow channel of clear and cold water starting at 0.2 mile. Soon after, note an eroded and steep cliff face on the other shore at 0.8 mile; look for the 20-foot-tall, rare Pacific yew (redwood-like needles) at trailside. Shortly, you'll see but not hear a fast-moving sheet of white just beyond a big rock outcrop so imposing it causes the course of the river to veer.

Set in a steep and rocky canyon dotted with majestic Douglas firs, rectangular-shaped Middle Falls are some 30 yards wide with a spectacular drop-off half that number. The trail then snakes up and away from the river, reaches a prime vista down on the Middle Falls, ascends some long, wooden steps, and culminates on a rocky rim. From a nearby rocky perch beneath a cluster of ponderosa pines, check out a clear view of the falls setting.

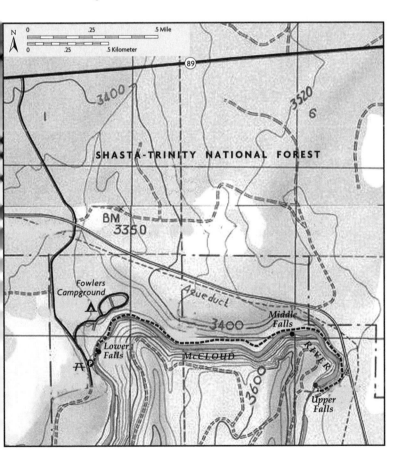

The surging white water in the canyon resembles a wild scene from the Colorado River. Look forward to pleasing views of Mount Shasta and mountains of the Trinity Divide along this stretch of the return route. More inspirational and longing looks down into the river continue for another 0.25 mile or so. At 1.4 miles you reach a shady section featuring a staggeringly steep wall of lichen-coated gray rock on the left side of the trail. The first sighting of the Upper Falls promptly ensues just past this 20-foot-high corridor.

Hemmed in on both sides by steep granite cliffs, these falls are an extremely powerful chute of pure white water. Looking down on the rushing water, it's easy to imagine a bursting dam. Make your way down the spur trail to the edge of a large and round swirling pool (ideal for trout fishing).

5. Mount Eddy and Deadfall Lakes

Round trip: 9 miles
Hiking time: 6 hours or overnight
High point: 9025 feet
Elevation gain: 2850 feet
Best hiking time: Early July through mid-October
Water: From lakes and streams, none past Upper Deadfall Lake
Maps: USGS Mount Eddy, USGS South China
Contact: Shasta-Trinity National Forest, Mount Shasta Ranger District, (530) 926-4511

Getting there: Drive 3.4 miles north of the community of Weed and take the Edgewood/Gazelle exit. Go under the freeway, turn right at the stop sign, and take a signed left at Stewart Springs Road at 0.3 mile. At 4.7 miles, turn right onto Forest Road 17, known also as the Parks Creek Road. Follow this winding, often one-lane paved path 13.7 miles to Parks Creek Pass and the Deadfall Lakes parking area.

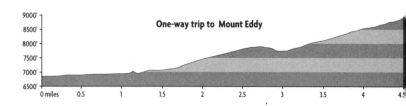

Majestic Mount Shasta from the top of 9025-foot Mount Eddy.

Most people in the north state give snowmelt from the flanks of Mount Eddy the nod as the headwaters of the Sacramento River, at 384 miles the longest river in California. One look from the windswept, flattened top of this peak, and who's to argue?

There's no argument when it comes to shouldering a pack into the Deadfall Lakes Basin, where man and beast can find cool, clear waters to swim, and humans can chase rainbow and brook trout in Lower and Middle Deadfall Lakes. This is a great destination for families with younger children, since the trail gains little elevation to and from the basin. It's the hike to the peak that will have adventurers wheezing.

The trail begins to the west of the parking area (just past the information kiosk). You'll be following the Pacific Crest Trail into the basin, which stays wide and level through a forest of red and white fir, ponderosa, and Jeffery pine and shady patches of yarrow and dwarf larkspur.

At about a mile, you'll cross a seasonal creek, and hit another gurgling spring at about 1.8 miles up the trail, just before reaching the stunning Deadfall Meadows. The wildflower display lasts well into summer, with sage, yellow lupine, white-flowered angelica, corn lily, and red columbine. Western white fir dominates the landscape until the path crosses a burbling Deadfall Creek, where there's a signed crossroads. Go right and you'll soon reach the swimmable waters of Lower Deadfall Lake, where a few campsites beckon. Turn left and you'll be following the historic Sisson-Callahan Trail, along which Middle Deadfall Lake awaits to the right.

The emerald-green waters of Middle Deadfall Lake make for a wonderful base camp to attack the summit of Mount Eddy. Fantastic campsites lie on the lake's west and northern shores (fishing for rainbow and brook trout also is at its best here).

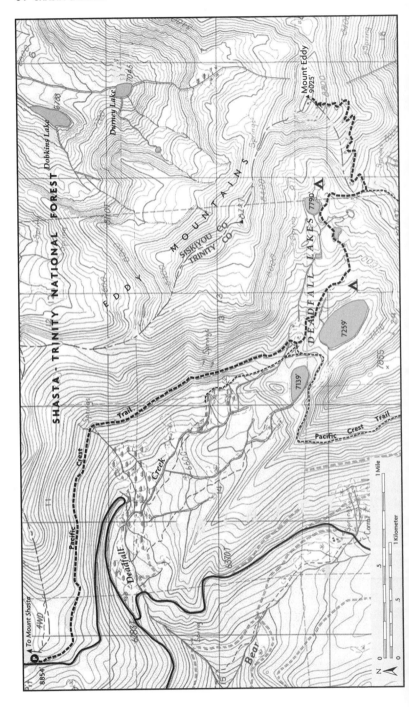

At 3.1 miles, you'll reach the first of three ponds where you can purify water for the last push up to the summit. At 3.3 miles, you'll reach Upper Deadfall Lake and get the awesome view of this trek's prize—the red-stained rocks of Mount Eddy. Continue climbing to Mount Eddy Pass for a commanding view of the Deadfall Basin, the whole of the Trinity Alps, and Lake Siskiyou.

Go left at the signed trail fork, where you'll climb relentlessly on switchbacks for another 0.7 mile. Just when you think you've run out of breath, you'll gain sight of a jumbled pile of wood—the remnants of an old fire lookout—and the summit of Mount Eddy.

Here's where, surprisingly, you'll get your first glimpse of Mount Shasta since leaving the trailhead. Officially, the high point of the peak is a wind-swept corner on the western edge. Hikers have built a rock circle around the high point.

6. Castle Dome

Round trip: 5.8 miles
Hiking time: 3 hours
High point: 4700 feet
Elevation gain: 1750 feet
Best hiking time: Early April through mid-November
Water: Best to bring your own, and lots of it
Maps: USGS Dunsmuir, USFS Castle Crags Wilderness
Contact: Castle Crags State Park, (530) 235-2684

Getting there: Take the Castle Crags State Park/Castella exit off Interstate 5 and follow the signs west to the park's entrance. Turn right and take the main paved road through the campground, following the signs for photography and the vista point. It's another winding mile from the campground to the trailhead.

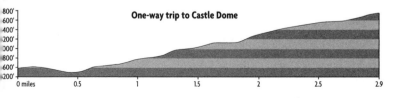

One-way trip to Castle Dome

The day hikers stopped along the sun-beaten path beneath the towering spires of Castle Crags to gawk at the lone dusty hiker coming down the path.

In Castle Crags State Park, those out for the day often mingle with the thru-hikers completing the 2650-mile Pacific Crest Trail. It's a place where campers with kids out for a weekend of fun can share a meal and a story with someone making the months-long trek from Mexico to Canada.

The park also offers swimming and fishing along the upper Sacramento River, hiking in the backcountry, and grand views of Mount Shasta from the exciting Castle Dome Trail. There's a great waterfall (Burstarse Falls) and cool springs to recharge the water bottles. There's also the 6000-foot glacier-polished granite spires that give the park its name.

In short, this 4350-acre state park near Castella is a mixed bag of uses, from day hikes or a cool weekend retreat to an area where people pass through on their way to points north or south. For the adventurous, the hike to the base of Castle Dome is a rite of passage.

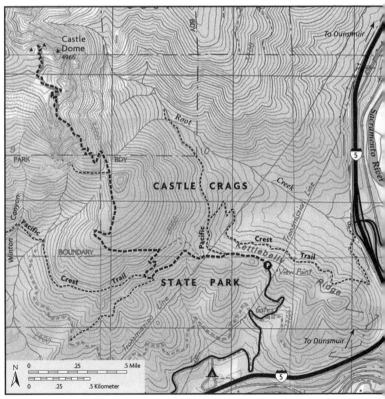

The granitic wonders of Castle Crags from a bridge above Castle Creek

Since the dome lies within the Castle Crags Wilderness Area, dogs are allowed on the trail. But please be aware that dogs must be on a leash within Castle Crags State Park.

The trail begins to the right, about 150 feet down the road from the parking area. At 0.25 mile, there's a trail junction where you'll want to go left and where you'll start this arduous climb under a canopy of dense fir and pine. It doesn't let up until you reach the base of Castle Dome.

At 0.5 mile, you'll join up with the PCT briefly until you take a signed trail to the right. Go right again at another trail fork at 1 mile, where you'll get the first glimpses of the grand granite spires. Knowing what's ahead will keep you going as you take on this vigorous climb. At 2 miles, a path heads left a short distance to Indian Springs, the last sure watering hole on the path to the dome.

After almost 3 miles of climbing, you'll reach the base of Castle Dome, where you'll gain views of Mount Shasta, Girard Ridge, Grey Ridge, Shasta Bally, and Bully Choop. A note about the dome: Many people choose to climb to the top. Do so only if you have rock-climbing experience, have shoes with a gripping tread, and dry rock on which to climb.

And remember, your four-legged pal won't be able to make it, so be happy you conquered this uphill devil in the first place.

7. Bailey Cove Loop

Round trip: 2.5-mile loop
Hiking time: 2 hours
High point: 1150 feet
Elevation gain: 400 feet
Best hiking time: Year-round
Water: From Lake Shasta
Map: USGS O'Brien
Contact: Shasta-Trinity National Forest, Shasta Lake Ranger District, (530) 275-1589

Getting there: Take the Shasta Caverns Road exit off Interstate 5, about 15 miles north of Redding. Drive east 0.4 mile and turn right onto Bailey Cove Road. Drive 0.7 mile to where the road ends, and pick up the trail near the water's edge (it's signed Bailey Cove Loop). The trail begins in a clockwise direction from a large canyon live oak and some smallish ponderosa pine.

Mix equal parts of rambunctious dog, fishing rod, brilliant fall afternoon, and a family and you've got a tonic called Bailey Cove Loop.

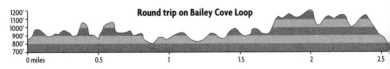

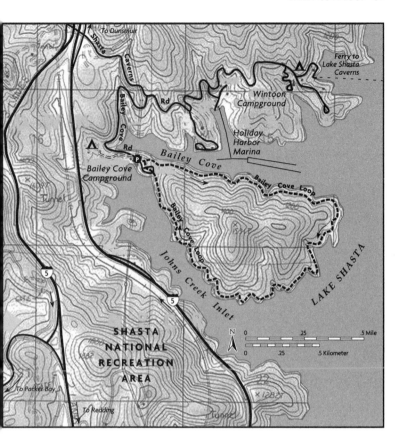

This trail takes in a few miles of shoreline of California's largest man-made lake. Lake Shasta was created when Shasta Dam was built in 1945, harnessing the waters of the Sacramento, McCloud, and Pit Rivers. The lake has 365 miles of shoreline, one for every day of the year.

Here, you'll get to explore a prominent peninsula that once was a mountain. This well-maintained trail attracts anglers who sling lines into the numerous coves, as well as mountain bikers and families out for a stroll. You'll get a glimpse of Holiday Harbor, one of the many marinas that cater to the myriad of houseboaters who make annual pilgrimages to the lake.

Commanding the view is 3114-foot-high North Gray Rocks. This limestone formation houses the splendor of the renowned Lake Shasta Caverns (*www.lakeshastacaverns.com*), where people can take a boat ride across the lake and get a peek at the water-created formations in the

Limestone formations across from Bailey Cove, winter (photo by Marc Soares)

cave. Limestone, it should be noted, is the compressed skeletal remains of marine life that lived more than 200 million years ago. This soft rock is transformed into elegant calcite crystal formations.

This mostly flat trail is tantalizingly close to the water's edge, and you'll have a hard time getting the dogs to stay on the trail—mine love to swim along—as the footpath swings south out of the cove through gnarled whiteleaf manzanita. In the few sunny spots, poison oak grows tall and lush, so beware and make sure to wash your dog off before she climbs back into your car.

At 1.3 miles, the trail meanders under a grove of knobcone pine and reaches a gulch with easy access to a small cove. Move past a collection of common mullein plants (marked by large, gray fans for leaves) to a flat space to swim and have a snack.

You'll find plenty of secluded lakeside perches on this trail. The final mile loops above the cove formed by the Johns Creek Inlet and affords the sunniest locations on this trek. You'll find the canyon live oaks here grow like shrubs.

8. Waters Gulch Creek to Packers Bay

Round trip: 3.7-mile loop
Hiking time: 4 hours
High point: 1400 feet
Elevation gain: 1100 feet
Best hiking time: Year-round
Water: From Lake Shasta
Map: USGS O'Brien
Contact: Shasta-Trinity National Forest, Shasta Lake Ranger District, (530) 275-1589

Getting there: From Interstate 5 north, about 15 miles north of Redding, take the Shasta Caverns/Packers Bay exit. Drive under the freeway and get back on I-5 going south. Drive 1 mile and take the Packers Bay exit. Turn right, drive 1 mile, and park in the small paved lot.

A buddy of mine begged me not to include this hike in this guide. "Awwww, let's just keep it for ourselves," he said. "And the dogs."

Sorry, but this is one great hike, a chance to see the Sacramento Arm of Lake Shasta up close and personal, all the while giving the hounds a chance to run off all that pent-up intensity. There's even the chance to explore Waters Gulch Creek, a slight waterway that loses its intensity during the summer, but comes crashing back in the winter.

Here is where the lake takes a slight departure from the surrounding forest. The hike goes through a black oak forest, which is California's most colorful oak. In spring and early summer, its leaves are as green as the waters of Lake Shasta; in the fall, whole hillsides turn a mix of orange and yellow. And thanks to my guide-writing friend, Marc Soares, I now know to look for the recently discovered Shasta snow wreath, which is a shrub in the rose family.

From the onset, you'll get a good workout getting to the top of the

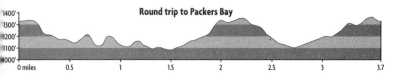

Round trip to Packers Bay

Where there's water, there should be dogs. Trinity gets ready to get wet at Lake Shasta.

Overlook Trail, so named because it offers a secluded look at the crown jewel of the Central Valley Water Project: Lake Shasta.

Descend the mostly shaded 0.5-mile trail and head for the signed Waters Gulch Trail, which promptly leads to its namesake creek. The north slope is festooned with Douglas fir, no doubt drinking heartily on the moisture afforded the slope. Here, you'll find a slender spur trail that will lead you to a small but powerful waterfall. The falls are protected by a fragrant grove of California bay laurel trees, adding to your enjoyment of the rushing waters.

To find a clear pool at the end of the falls, walk another 100 yards down the main trail. Be careful when climbing down a small side trail, where a tiny seasonal creek on the opposite shore topples into Waters Gulch Creek and into the lake. If the lake is full, you can swim some 20 yards and soak in the tiny whirlpools created by the falls. As an added bonus, there's plenty of flat boulders on which to sun yourself and maybe take in a snack.

Get back on the trail and you'll find yourself in a sea of dogwoods, bigleaf maple, and alder. The scene shifts from crashing waters to a more serene setting where the trail follows the wooded shoreline and wood boards cross babbling streams that lead to driftwood-strewn coves. Everything is cool and green, which allows the mind to wander and the soul to be freed.

At 2.2 miles, the trail begins to climb inland under black oak to a wooden bench at 2.7 miles. Here your lake views disappear, replaced by steep west and southern slopes packed with chaparral plants, mostly gray pine and scruffy canyon live oaks. The trail meets another stream at 3.2 miles.

After crossing another brook, look for the signed, but overgrown, Fish Loop Trail, which is used by anglers to get to prime points out in Packers Bay. Compared to the ups and downs of the Packers Bay Trail, the Fish Loop Trail is an easily flayed 0.5-mile loop that really doesn't offer much in the way of views. However, bank anglers can catch a stringer of bass or trout (depending on the time of year) from the many lake access points.

From the start of the Fish Loop Trail, retrace your steps, walk to the access road to Packers Bay Marina, and climb another 0.5 mile to your vehicle.

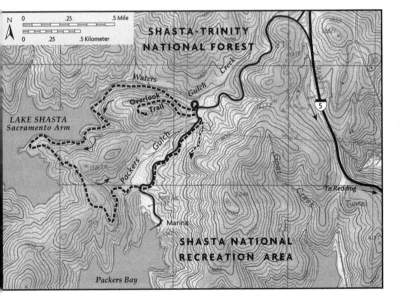

9. Clikapudi Trail

Round trip: 6.8-mile loop; 4.2 miles out-and-back to Clikapudi Bay
Hiking time: 3–6 hours
High point: 1300 feet
Elevation gain: 700 feet
Best hiking time: Year-round
Water: From Lake Shasta, or Jones Valley Boat Ramp
Map: USGS Millville
Contact: Shasta-Trinity National Forest, Shasta Lake Ranger District, (530) 275-1589

Getting there: Take Highway 299 east from Redding and drive 6 miles to the community of Bella Vista. Turn north on Dry Creek Road and drive 6.8 miles to the Y with Jones Valley Road. Veer right and drive 1.2 miles to a small gravel parking lot on the left, just past the 25-mile-per-hour sign. The trail starts next to the sign.

The Jones Fire flared early in the morning on October 16, 1999, near Lake Shasta's Clikapudi Trail. Driven by 50-mile-per-hour winds, the fire roared through Jones Valley, Bella Vista, and Palo Cedro. By the time it was stopped, it had gone nearly 26 miles—stretching almost to the Sacramento River in Anderson. The fire also damaged this multiuse trail, which was closed to everyone until late 2000.

Fortunately, the Forest Service has been diligent, and this trail is again attracting everyone from families and their dogs to fishermen and mountain bikers. Yes, this is a popular destination, but in the off-season (October through May) you and your dog can find the kind of seclusion many millionaires pay top price to achieve.

This well-constructed trail meanders past Wintu Indian archaeological sites, along with great samples of native plants and trees. In early spring and late fall, the trail is fairly shaded; in winter and spring, you'll encounter many intimate creeks that feed this 30,000-acre lake.

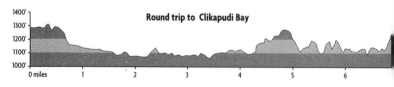

Round trip to Clikapudi Bay

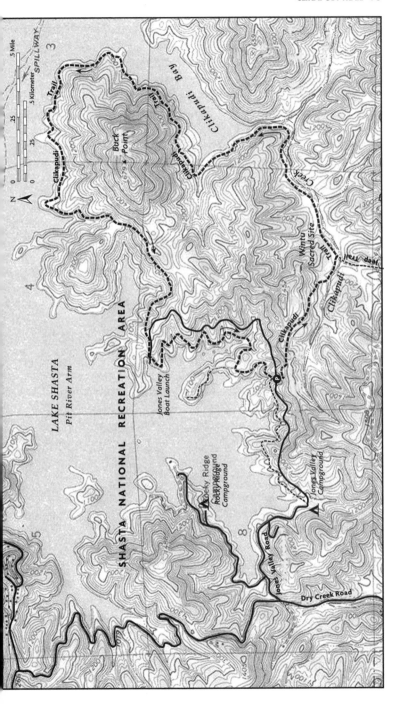

Clikapudi Creek, mid-winter (photo by Marc Soares)

During the summer months, it's best to have the dogs on leashes, lest you want entanglements with surprised anglers and mountain bikers completing the twisted path, rated as a Top 10 single-track destination in California ("single-track" because the path is just wide enough to accommodate one rider).

You'll see why this is single-track heaven for mountain bikers. From the get-go, this yard-wide path climbs nearly 0.5 mile through a woodland of black oaks, ponderosa pine, massively gnarled whiteleaf manzanita, and gray pine. It then heads down into a narrow slot that stays close to a seasonal stream.

At 0.9 mile, go left as the trail joins an old jeep road. A sign on a fencepost announces the sacred Wintu site (it's all protected, so please stay out) and then crosses Clikapudi Creek. You'll reach a second sacred Wintu site at 1.2 miles.

Another 0.5 mile along the trail, you'll notice how Clikapudi Creek gets deeper, faster, and stronger as it enters Clikapudi Bay. Just past the inlet, there's a grove of willows that makes for a great spot to take a dip, sling a line, and generally relax—a reward for making it this far.

Continue on and you'll get to a wooden bridge that crosses a driftwood-strewn, quiet inlet cove at 2.2 miles. You'll notice how the bay gets noticeably bigger at the third feeder stream at 2.7 miles. The area is full of wild California grapevines. At the fourth and fifth feeder streams, the water pours over solid rock.

Pass through some scrubby canyon live oak and whiteleaf manzanita to a vista point that overlooks twin peninsulas and a curvaceous spot along the lake's Pit River Arm at 3.6 miles. The trail now swings around another driftwood-strewn inlet stream at 4.2 miles and that's where you'll pick up the mixed knobcone, ponderosa, and Douglas-fir forest. The trail will hug the shore, allowing for numerous dunks into the lake for the dogs. You'll find plenty of driftwood to toss out for hounds that like to fetch.

At 5 miles, at the union of two seasonal creeks, the trail climbs out of the canyon and up to the Jones Valley Boat Ramp parking lot, where there's water and public restrooms. Continue on the trail past the parking lot, pass a few more coves that will give you views to the damage that the fire caused, and—finally—you'll come back to where you started.

10. Boulder Creek Falls

Round trip: 4.8 miles
Hiking time: 3 hours or overnight
High point: 2250 feet
Elevation gain: 1000 feet
Best hiking time: Year-round; streams might not be passable in early spring
Water: From Boulder Creek
Map: USGS French Gulch
Contact: Whiskeytown National Recreation Area, Whiskeytown Unit, (530) 246-1225 or (530) 242-3400

Getting there: Take Highway 299 west from Redding about 10 miles (and 2 miles past the Oak Bottom Campground turnoff) and turn left onto Judge Francis Carr Powerhouse Road. After 0.3 mile past the powerplant, the road becomes the dirt South Shore Drive. You'll reach a crossroads at 2.3 miles, where there's room to park along the shoulder of the road. The trail is beyond a gate, but you'll recognize it, as this trek is popular with both hikers and mountain bikers.

This hike leads, arguably, to the prettiest waterfall in Whiskeytown National Recreation Area: a spectacular 120-foot drop that changes its attitude with the changing seasons. Better still, the best vantage point of the falls is on a mossy granite slab across the ridge from where Boulder Creek begins its tumble to Whiskeytown Lake.

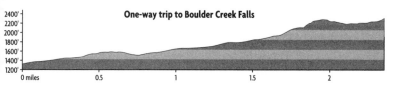

By late winter and early spring, the falls are at their most frothy white, and be prepared to get a little wet on the three stream crossings on the way to the falls. But in summer, when the temperatures are hovering around 100 degrees, cool, inviting Boulder Creek is a hiker's delight, with many pools that teem with tiny rainbow trout and native sculpin, a small bottom-dwelling fish.

If you've never had a backcountry experience with your pet, here's the place to change that, all while being little more than 10 miles from the heart of Redding. Along the way to the falls are two seldom-used backcountry campsites, shaded in oak and pine forest, within the harmonious sounds of the creek rushing over granite boulders.

The trail starts off along an old fire road, where you should keep a sharp eye out for the numerous fence lizards and the occasional alligator lizard. A treat, if they are out sunning themselves, are the beautiful (and harmless) California mountain king snakes. This cream/black/red-striped reptile is a natural enemy of the rattlesnake and sometimes is confused with the deadly poisonous coral snake (which has yellow/black/red bands). This

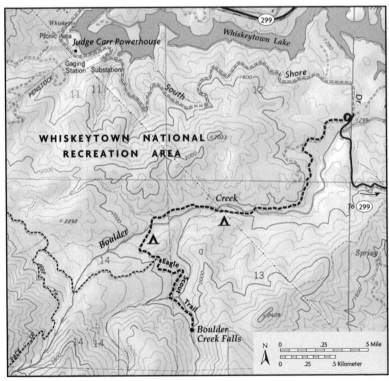

trail is the only one in Whiskeytown where I've ever seen king snakes. Please don't let your dogs get too curious, as the king snake will still snap at a curious, wet nose.

The trail climbs steadily for nearly a mile, where a seasonal creek joins Boulder Creek and your first stream crossing. Soon, you'll pass the first trailside campsite. Traveling on, you'll come up on two gigantic sugar pines, by far the largest species of pine on this hike, and the second stream crossing. The trail will veer from the creek after the third crossing, where you'll reach the second campsite and the site of an old homestead. This is a great place to stop for lunch and walk around and imagine what it would have been like to live—and work—in such beautiful surroundings.

Shasta Bally, at 6209 feet in elevation, looms close (its snowmelt feeds Boulder Creek) just before the trail descends toward the final creek

My daughter, Jessica Yegge, and Scully meander down the Boulder Creek Falls Trail with snow-capped Shasta Bally in the background.

crossing at 2.3 miles. Look for a signed trailhead to the left that begins an ascent up old stairs made from surrounding pine. This was an Eagle Scout project that, for now, has stood the test of time. Climb the twisting stairs until you reach the granite boulder, big enough for two people and two dogs, and take a moment to listen to the rushing sounds of the falls.

The falls are adorned by bigleaf maples. Actually, Boulder Creek Falls is a series of three drops. The highest falls cascade into the middle falls, which plummet into a pool surrounded by slick, mossy rocks. Water then spills over and drops 75 feet into a deep, clear, sandy-bottomed pool.

Retrace your steps back to your car, or you have the option of continuing along the fire road (at the base of the Eagle Scout Trail) and continuing west toward Mill Creek Road, where it is possible to link up with the Mill Creek Trail (Hike 11).

11. Mill Creek Trail

Round trip: 5 miles or more
Hiking time: 2 hours
High point: 2050 feet
Elevation gain: 800 feet
Best hiking time: Year-round, but stream might not be passable in early spring
Water: From Mill Creek
Map: USGS French Gulch
Contact: Whiskeytown National Recreation Area, Whiskeytown Unit, (530) 246-1225 or (530) 242-3400

Getting there: Take Highway 299 west from Redding some 10 miles to a signed parking area for the Tower House Historic District on the south side of the highway. The parking area is just east of the bridge over Clear Creek, which is 0.1 mile east of French Gulch Road and 1.3 miles west of the Judge Francis Carr Powerhouse turn.

It's early evening on the Mill Creek Trail, but it sure seems a lot later. Broken sunlight filters through the oak and pine down to where I sit along a deep cut in the hillside.

The dogs are smart—they've found the pool and are hunkered down in the water at snout level. It's Africa-hot in the canyon, even though I'm parked just a few feet from the water's edge. My shirt moves to the beat of my heaving chest, as it's sweat-soaked and sticks to me from the collar down. Rivulets of sweat track down my face, and blowing air from my mouth makes a tiny fountain of salty water.

The sweat is the result of my pack, which holds one of those square plastic 2.5-gallon water jugs and an apple. It's also because I've walked the roughly 2.5-mile trail to a deep pool that is the turnaround point for this hike. This is the trail that has served as my physical therapy after knee surgery.

Certainly, the trail holds more than a punishing workout. It's completely shaded, the trail crosses Mill Creek eighteen times in 1.2 miles,

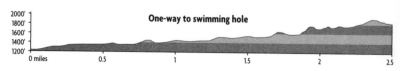

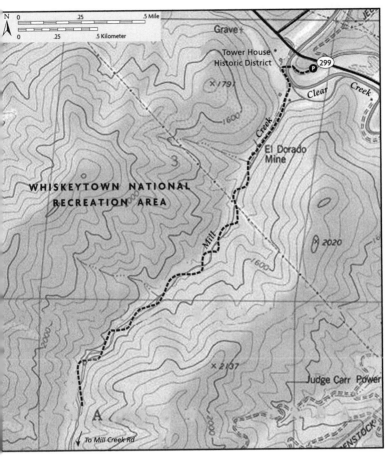

and the creek holds several pools where the dogs can rest. You'll also get a good look at how nature remakes itself, seeing how the old mining operation has been reclaimed by the land.

A note about poison oak: There's a ton of it on this hike. Make sure you've got a supply of over-the-counter soap in the car to wash yourself off, and be sure to dip the dogs in the waters of Clear Creek before hopping back in your car. My wife and I couldn't figure out how we kept breaking out in an itch and red rash a week after coming back from Mill Creek. The oils from the plant had been transferred to the dogs' fur, which kept getting transferred to us. It took two shots of steroids to get rid of the reaction.

After parking, go east toward the information kiosk, where you'll cross Clear Creek on an elegant footbridge, then do the same across Willow Creek. This sandy path leads you past the Camden House and meanders

Mill Creek's numerous boulder outcroppings are great for sunning yourself.

east toward a private home. The path then turns south, heading for the historic El Dorado Mine, a gold-mining operation that was active until 1967. Pass the mine and you'll see the wide trail narrow—and civilization starts drifting away.

After entering the shaded forest, you'll see your first chance at a swimming hole. If you can hold off, the swimming areas get better. A lot better. After just 2.5 miles of winding trail, you'll come upon one of the best, secluded swimming holes in California—a 15-foot-diameter, 5-foot-deep, sandy-bottomed soaking pool fed by a 5-foot, cascading waterfall. It's a place to rest, strip down, and take a dip. If only briefly. The water is sooooo clear and cold that it takes your breath away.

After a brief rest, it's time to retrace your steps to the car. This hike can be extended another 2.3 miles to Mill Creek Road, where you can meet up with the backside of the Boulder Creek Falls Trail (Hike 10).

12. Davis Gulch Trail

Round trip: 7 miles; 3.5 miles parking area to parking area
Hiking time: 3 hours
High point: 1500 feet
Elevation gain: 600 feet
Best hiking time: Year-round
Water: From the lake
Map: USGS French Gulch
Contact: Whiskeytown National Recreation Area, Whiskeytown Unit, (530) 246-1225 or (530) 242-3400

Getting there: From Redding, drive 8 miles west on Highway 299 to the Whiskeytown National Recreation Area visitor center and turn left onto

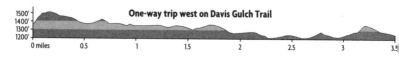

One-way trip west on Davis Gulch Trail

1500'
1400'
1300'
1200'

0 miles   0.5   1   1.5   2   2.5   3   3.5

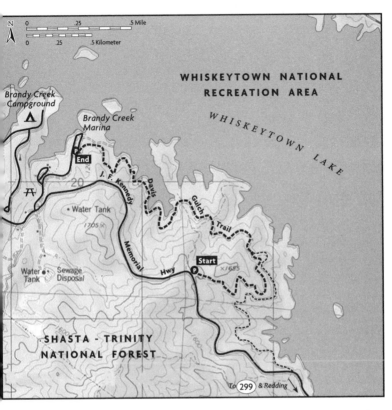

J. F. Kennedy Memorial Highway. Drive 1.6 miles and follow the road as it heads right over the Clair A. Hill/Whiskeytown Dam. The signed trailhead and dirt parking area is 1.1 miles from the dam.

No matter the time of year, the Davis Gulch Trail is a wonderful canopy of green that will refresh the soul and enhance the spirit. With the lake close by, there's also the chance to soak in a secluded bay, chase sticks, and generally take it easy.

Numerous gulches bring water to this trail, which meanders down to the lake, then comes out near the bathrooms at the Brandy Creek Marina. If 3.5 miles is all you care to do, you could definitely car shuttle on this hike, but an out-and-back trip is worth the extra steps, especially when the water's warm and you can take a dip with the dogs midway back to the car. Each turn brings a new and exciting feature for hikers. One gulch may be filled with the sounds of water rushing over boulders; the next will have you gazing at a moss-covered rock wall.

The Davis Gulch Trail is a study in shapes and colors, as this gnarled manzanita bush proves.

Overhead, you might catch a glimpse of the breeding pair of bald eagles that nest in the area; certainly, the resident osprey and turkey vulture populations will be cruising the thermals above the lake. Tread quietly, and you'll likely see all manner of mammals and reptiles. Fence lizards are common, skittering off in the fallen, crisp leaves from the resident live oaks. Bears are known to use the trail, as are deer and the occasional raccoon and opossum.

All along the trail, park service staff have built cozy wooden benches for relaxing and taking in the sights and there are twenty interpretive signs along the trail. At just 0.75 mile, a sign tells hikers about the canyon live oaks that dot the landscape. The brass sign sits in front of a gnarled live oak with a large root system that somehow has managed to affix to the shallow soil covering a stretch of boulder. Other signs point out the resident flora, including holly, manzanita, poison oak, ponderosa, and gray pine.

At about 1.5 miles, you'll come to a thicket of Brewer oak. The sign tells of this transplant from Oregon and how it helps anchor the soil and prevent erosion. Farther along, you'll come to an opening that affords a panorama of Whiskeytown Lake, part of the Whiskeytown National Recreation Area. The lake, filled in 1963, stores water for both power and irrigation in the Central Valley.

At about 2 miles, you'll come to a cove, where the dogs can take on water and take a swim. While it's somewhat of a steep drop from the trail, there are two pathways that lead man and beast to the cove's emerald-green waters, which are protected by two islands in the distance.

At 2.5 miles, you'll come upon an old mine cave that's been filled in (it's on the other side of the cove). After another mostly level mile, you'll come to the Brandy Creek Marina parking lot, where the trail conveniently passes the restrooms. After a short rest and a chance to refill the water bladder, it's time to backtrack to your car.

13. Kanaka Peak

Round trip: 7.8-mile loop
Hiking time: 6 hours
High point: 2700 feet
Elevation gain: 1700 feet
Best hiking time: Year-round; midsummer heat might be a problem
Water: From Paige Boulder Creek, but pack plenty
Map: USGS French Gulch
Contact: Whiskeytown National Recreation Area, Whiskeytown
Unit, (530) 246-1225 or (530) 242-3400

Getting there: From Redding, drive 8 miles west on Highway 299 to the Whiskeytown National Recreation Area visitor center and turn left onto J. F. Kennedy Memorial Highway. Drive about 2 miles, to where the road splits across the dam. Continue south on Paige Bar Road. After 1 mile,

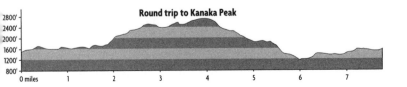

Round trip to Kanaka Peak

Whiskeytown Lake is framed by Shasta Bally, right, and Kanaka Peak, left.

turn right onto the dirt road, which is Peltier Valley Road. The road crosses a bridge, goes up for 1.7 miles, and then crosses a seasonal stream. Park in the clearing.

While it isn't nearly as tall as its neighbor to the north—the 6209-foot Shasta Bally, which dominates Redding's western vistas—Kanaka Peak is no slouch of a hike. It's strenuous, to be sure, but the views of Whiskeytown Lake, the snowcapped Klamath Mountains (even in the middle of summer), and the Central Valley are not to be missed.

Besides, you'll be walking the dogs through history, as the area was very important to the resident Wintu Indians who gathered acorns for flour, hunted deer, and took salmon, trout, and steelhead from the creeks. Of course, the Wintu had a much different view from Kanaka Peak. Whereas you'll see 3000-acre Whiskeytown Lake and urban sprawl from an expanding Redding and the rest of the Central Valley, they saw expansive forest and grasslands. Alas, along the way, you'll also see the scars of years of gold exploration, where miners dug gullies and trenches—and aided in the rapid decline of the Native Americans.

When the rains come in the winter and through the spring, you'll have the chance to view a gushing waterfall and water cascading over the boulders in Paige Boulder Creek. Hike in the fall, and the scene changes: the creek still babbles happily on, but you'll have the added bonus of some of the best fall color in the north state, as the dogwoods, black oak, and maple go all warm shades.

To start the hike, cross Paige Boulder Creek on giant granite boulders and turn up the unsigned Kanaka Peak Loop Trail. The path follows the gin-clear waters of Paige Boulder Creek for about 100 yards, then veers upward into a forest of canyon live oak, black oak, and ponderosa pine.

One mile in on the way up Kanaka Peak, you'll come to a slight trail that is one of several side trails that can be used to extend your trip. This particular trail goes about 0.5 mile through dense timber—you'll swear you've returned to the time of the Wintu—and comes to a crashing, 15-foot-tall waterfall that pours over a solid piece of granite. There are plenty of granite boulders to climb on, from which perches you can watch the flow of Paige Boulder Creek and forget all your worldly troubles.

Just a little ways past the side trail, you'll get the first look at your destination, Kanaka Peak, which in the Wintu language, means "gold." You'll cross the stream again, then the trail climbs steeply and eventually hooks

up with a ridge with great views of the lake below. Here, you'll come to a leaning canyon live oak that towers over the sign announcing the recreation area's boundary. Rest here, since there's still a climb of nearly 0.5 mile more to the top (you'll know you're almost there when you get to the giant sugar pine). And don't be fooled by the steep descent from the boundary sign.

Once you've made it around the thicket of manzanita and canyon live oak bushes, stop to take in the views: Mount Shasta to the north, the radio and television towers on Shasta Bally, the jagged peaks of the Trinity Alps, the Yolla Bolla Mountains to the south, and Lassen Peak and Chaos Crags to the east.

In 1991, the area was swept by fire. You'll continue downward through this burn area, where you'll get to see the impact fire has on the landscape. Pine and oak punches through the ground cover; if you're lucky, you'll be treated to deer feeding on all this developing vegetation.

Keep dropping down steeply (and watch out for mountain bikers; the trail also is very popular with downhillers who have nicknamed the ride "The Recliner"), boulder-hop Paige Boulder Creek, and then follow the stream to the trailhead.

14. Arboretum Perimeter Trail

Round trip: 1.8-mile loop
Hiking time: 1 hour
High point: 557 feet
Elevation gain: 206 feet
Best hiking time: Year-round
Water: Bring your own
Map: USGS Redding
Contact: City of Redding Community Services Division, (530) 225-4512

Getting there: From Redding heading north on Interstate 5, take the Lake Boulevard exit and turn left onto Lake. Drive 0.5 mile to the stoplight to

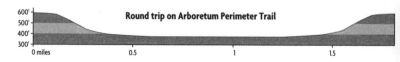

Round trip on Arboretum Perimeter Trail

access Hilltop Drive. Turn left onto Hilltop and drive 1 mile to the trailhead, which is signed with a large concrete sign. Just park off the street.

It's just a wisp of a trail, based on north state standards, but the McConnell Arboretum Perimeter Trail packs a wallop for dog walkers, mountain bikers, and fitness striders.

It's been a few years in the making—and as of July 4, 2004 it's connected to the nearly 12-mile Sacramento River Trail (Hike 15)—but the nearly 2-mile trail is a fantastic place to take a leisurely stroll. Construction near the Sundial Bridge that links Turtle Bay Exploration Park with the McConnell Arboretum blocks the opening of the perimeter trail from the rest of the river trail (the $24-million bridge, designed by famed architect Santiago Calatrava, opened to the public in the summer of 2004).

Before construction on the bridge began, a temporary footbridge was placed over Sulphur Creek, which empties into the Sacramento at the base of the Sundial Bridge. It was taken out when construction began in earnest, thus cutting off the trail from the arboretum parking lot and the rest of the river trail. It became the trail that most of Redding forgot, until people learned to access the trail from Hilltop Drive, through a former burn dump that was cleaned up and a 0.5-mile winding Hilltop Extension that drops into the river bottom.

Years back, the perimeter trail was a refuge for mountain bikers and dog lovers; they tore around on the old, decomposed granite surface. Through a cooperative effort among Turtle Bay, the McConnell Foundation, Redding East Rotary, Daniel Cook Industries, Tullis and Heller Inc., Coyote and Fox Enterprises, CH2M Hill, Construction Products Inc., and Sacramento Watershed Action Group, the new surface is a civilized improvement. In 1998, a layer of base rock was put down, then the trail was paved and linked to the Hilltop Extension. The trail had its official "coming out" party in 2000, during American Trails' National Trails Symposium.

From the trailhead, corkscrew down to the river bottom (it's a great workout going back up—the extension gains 206 feet in a 0.5 mile) and either turn left or right. Left takes you close to the river, while going right will take you through oak-studded hills. If you walk briskly, you can complete the entire loop in 45 minutes.

Nothing beats a quick stroll through the oak groves and riparian habitat. And if you've got the time, there's always the chance to stop and watch

Seasonal Sulphur Creek, which hosts spawning salmon and steelhead in the fall, is a great place to relax and take in the sights.

the river flow by, with all sorts of waterfowl feeding and the chance salmon and trout willing to break the water surface. Red-shouldered hawks squeal overhead and all manner of songbirds flitter from tree branch to tree branch. After watching a hawk swoop down and take a field mouse from the trail's edge, I watched a covey of California quail go waddling off into the brush, more than twenty little teardrop plumes bobbling along.

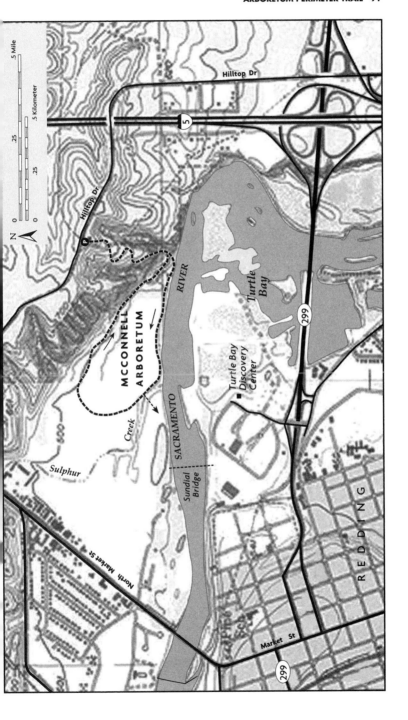

The perimeter trail is a work in progress. Still in the plans are drinking fountains, a shady area with picnic tables, and native landscaping for the winding Hilltop Extension. And, of course, when the bridge opens to the public sometime this year, the perimeter trail will finally be linked to the rest of the Sacramento River Trail by the existing green bridge across Sulphur Creek (where, in the spring, you still might be able to see salmon and steelhead spawning in the seasonal stream).

Runners, hikers, and bikers are already salivating at the prospects. Just think, in a few months, it will be possible to park your car on Hilltop Drive and walk the dogs all the way to the base of Shasta Dam, nearly 20 miles away.

15. Sacramento River Trail

Round trip: 6 miles
Hiking time: 2.5 hours
High point: 550 feet
Elevation gain: 50 feet
Best hiking time: Year-round
Water: At the trailhead
Map: USGS Redding
Contact: City of Redding Trails and Parks Department, (530) 224.6100

Getting there: From Interstate 5, take the Lake Boulevard exit (cross the river) and take an immediate right into the southside parking area. The trail starts behind the brown pipe gate, where dog walkers can pick up a plastic pooper-scooper bag.

If your impression of Redding is the choking gas fumes and fast-food neon along the busy Cypress Avenue exit off Interstate 5, then you're missing an oasis that is just a few miles from the bustle of the freeway.

Thank the City of Redding for having the foresight to incorporate the city's signature river—it cuts the city in half—into a recreation trail that is used by walkers, cyclists, roller skaters, kayakers, canoeists, and anglers.

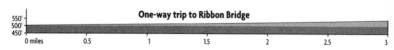

One-way trip to Ribbon Bridge

The Sacramento River Trail, which the city plans to extend once the Santiago Calatrava–designed Sundial Bridge is completed in the summer of 2004, won the American Trails Association's 2002 Best Trail Award. It is one of the last places along the Sacramento—at 377 miles California's longest river—where you can see the riparian forest as it was when the first settlers rode wagon trains to the water's edge.

From the parking area to the unique concrete ribbon footbridge that spans the river near Keswick Dam and along the north side of the trail to the historic Diestelhorst Bridge (built in 1918) and back to the parking area is 6.8 miles; this hike highlights the southside trail to the ribbon bridge and back, which is a 6-mile trip.

The trail is wide and inviting, with a thicket of alders, willows, oaks, Himalayan blackberry, live oak, and wildflowers coming right up to the asphalt.

The Sacramento River Trail (photo by Sharon Gabrukiewicz)

The trail is split so walkers traveling west stay on the right side, while people returning to the parking lot stay to the left. You're likely to hear, "Passing on your left," as cyclists come up to pass. Be courteous and take up the slack on the leash.

There are several good spots, with benches to rest, where the dogs can play in the waters of the Sacramento. Since it flows from the bottom of mighty Shasta Dam, the river stays at a chilly 52 degrees nearly year-round—refreshing for pets and nearly hypothermic for humans.

At 2 miles, you'll see a dirt path that leads to the right, while the trail turns left and gains its only true elevation of the hike. Take the dirt trail to a wide spot in the river, where clean gravel has been deposited to be washed down during the winter high flows for spawning salmon.

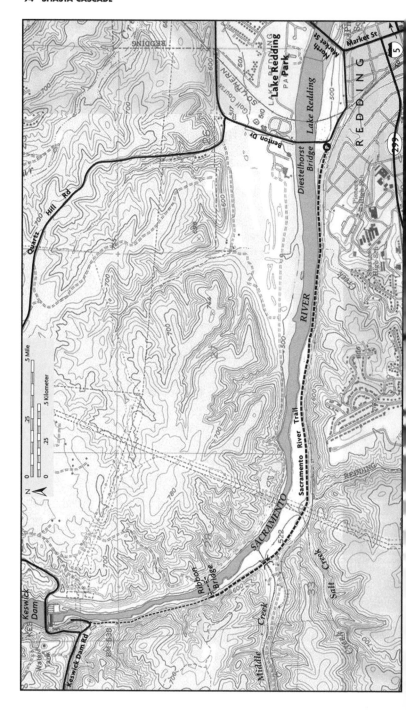

Back on the trail, you'll reach the historic Middle Creek Bridge, which is supported by hand-carved sandstone (and where rock climbers like to practice). After another 0.5 mile, you'll reach the ribbon bridge, built in 1990. The 13-foot-wide, 420-foot-long concrete stress-ribbon bridge is unique to this continent (this bridge type has been used in Czech Republic, Switzerland, and Germany) and has received a national award from the Portland Cement Association. The bridge hangs suspended from the banks of the river—there are no supports sunk into the water—nearly 30 feet above the emerald-green waters of the Sac.

It's a simple task to retrace your steps, stopping every so often to watch for river otters, osprey, bald eagles, snowy egrets, and other wildlife, while the dogs cool off in the river.

16. Blue Gravel Mine Trail

Round trip: 3.6 miles
Hiking time: 3 hours
High point: 200 feet
Elevation gain: 150 feet
Best hiking time: Year-round
Water: From one potable-water stop midway through the hike
Map: USGS Redding
Contact: City of Redding Trails and Parks Department,
    (530) 224-6100

Getting there: From Interstate 5, take the Cypress Avenue exit and turn left onto Cypress Avenue. Continue 1.4 miles until Cypress ends and turns into Market Street. Curve left onto south Market Street for 1.4 miles and turn left onto Buenaventura Boulevard. Drive 0.7 mile to the free parking area on the right side of the road.

Hats off to the folks in the City of Redding Trails and Parks Department, who for years have found the energy—and the money—to create new trails when other communities are struggling.

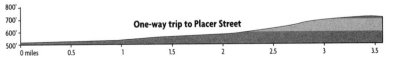

Redding and the surrounding federal lands that ring the town contain some of the best and varied trail systems around. But it's the exciting work the city is doing within its borders that gets hikers' attention. Here's what the city's website has to say:

> The City of Redding has embarked upon a local planning effort as it develops the Trails and Bikeway component of the Parks, Trails and Open Space Master Plan. The parkway, trails and greenway movement has evolved over time in Redding, with an initial focus on trails and trail recreation. However, a more comprehensive view is emerging. We now think of trails and bikeways as vital components of our community infrastructure. Redding's vision, articulated in many parts of the recently adopted 2000–2020 General Plan, describes an integrated system of parks and open spaces linked by its outstanding trails, bikeways and linear parks to each other, to schools, transit stops, residential neighborhoods, museums, the downtown and other major public attractions.

The Blue Gravel Mine Trail is exactly what city fathers have in mind. The first 1.8 miles of this trail are complete, and another mile of trail has

Hikers cross through a tunnel that cuts under Buenaventura Boulevard along the Blue Gravel Mine Trail in Redding.

been developed that will one day link the southwest part of the city with the sumptuous Sacramento River Trail (Hike 15).

This hike starts along busy Buenaventura Boulevard, crosses under the road by way of a metal tunnel, then heads into a canyon in which up until 1900, the city had exclusive rights to mine gold. Indeed, the canyon still holds relics from the area.

Once through the tunnel, you'll climb a bit and come to a water spigot that has its own dog dish. Refresh here, then press on toward the canyon, which is dotted with oak, gray pine, manzanita, and seasonal grasses. Of course, in spring the trail also comes alive with wildflowers—and the butterflies they attract.

The wide, paved trail continues up the canyon and away from any city noise. After leveling out slightly, the trail crosses a seasonal stream twice before coming to the terminus at a dirt parking area at the corner of Buenaventura Boulevard and Placer Street.

Rest a bit, then turn around and follow the trail downhill back to your car.

17. Magee Peak

Round trip: 12.6 miles
Hiking time: 2 days
High point: 8550 feet
Elevation gain: 3200 feet
Best hiking time: Mid-June through October; mosquitoes trouble-
some through July
Water: Only from Everett and Magee Lakes, or bring your own
Map: USGS Thousand Lakes Valley
Contact: Lassen National Forest, Hat Creek Ranger District, (530)
336-5521

Getting there: From Redding, go east on Highway 44/89 (44 turns int
89 near Lassen Volcanic National Park) and turn west onto Forest Roa
26, which begins 0.4 mile north of the Hat Creek Work Center and 1
miles south of Highway 299. Follow FR 26 for 7.5 miles—don't be tempte
by all the lesser logging and fire roads, stay on the signed road for FR 2(
Thousand Lakes Wilderness, and Cypress Camp. Turn left onto FR 34N6
and travel another 2.6 miles to the parking area, which is signed Thou
sand Lakes Wilderness Area–Cypress Camp.

The girls and I absolutely love cirque-surrounded, subalpine lakes. O
this hike, you'll pass two beautiful examples that are much less visite
than lakes in nearby Lassen Volcanic National Park—and you'll top ou
on one of Shasta County's Top 10 highest points.

To start, walk up the road, bear right and then left at two intersectior
within the first 200 yards of hiking, then cross Eiler Gulch Creek. You kno
you're on the right path—it's well-worn, as this is a popular weekend bacl
packing destination—as you start to climb southeast at a good clip, throug
a canopy of Jeffrey pine, white fir, and the occasional western juniper.

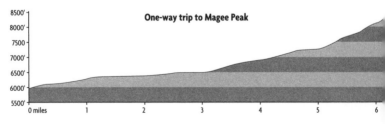

Lake Eiler's northeast shore near Magee Peak (photo by Marc Soares)

At 0.25 mile, you'll reach a trail junction; bear right, then right again at two other trail forks within 0.7 mile of hiking. You'll pass through an amazing display of flora, including tobacco brush, numerous wildflowers, lodgepole pine, red and white fir, and stubby pinemat manzanita.

Pine-encrusted Everett and Magee Lakes are about 2 miles farther from the last fork in the trail. Both lakes sit at 7200 feet in elevation. Both also offer good swimming and fishing opportunities—the lakes are stocked with fish every spring by airplane—and good camping spots. I prefer to stay at Magee Lake, since there's more room to spread out, as well as more campsites. Make sure if you're close to other campers that you have control of your dogs, and let people around you know you're hiking with animals. This just cuts down on any problems.

From the lakes, it's nearly another 2-mile push to the summit. To get here, pass by Magee Lake and bear right at the trail fork. As you climb, the canopy of pine opens, which allows fantastic views of the surrounding countryside. This is volcano country, meaning the surrounding rock is sharp and porous, meaning it's a good idea to pack your dog's booties.

At about 1.5 miles from the lake, you'll crest the ridge and then follow the trail another 0.3 mile to the summit, at 8550 feet elevation. Notice that you and your dog (or dogs) are standing on the rim of an ancient volcano that encompassed Peak 8446 (0.3 mile to the southeast), 8683-foot Crater Peak (0.5 mile north), and others. Though glaciers finished the contours of the Hat Creek area, it was volcanoes that first carved up the landscape.

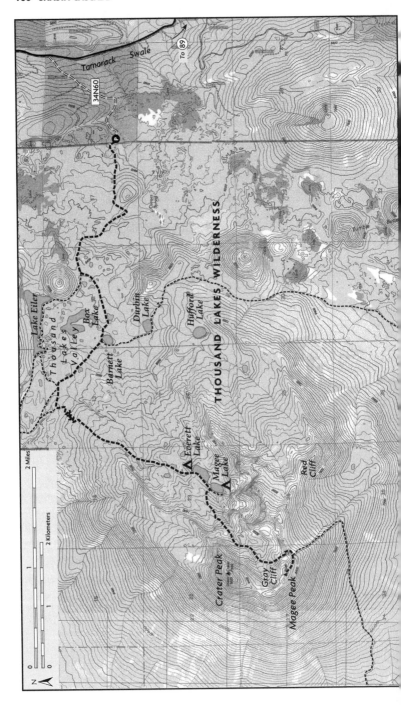

18. Baker Lake to Hat Creek Rim

Round trip: Up to 7 miles
Hiking time: 1–5 hours
High point: 5300 feet
Elevation gain: 500 feet
Best hiking time: Year-round; hot in the summer, a great snowshoe route
Water: Bring your own
Map: USGS Old Station
Contact: Lassen National Forest, Hat Creek Ranger District,
    (530) 336-5521

Getting there: From Redding, travel east on Highway 44. Park for free in the turnout near Forest Road 33N20, which is a few miles above the junction of Highways 89 and 44, northeast of the town of Old Station and 2.2 miles south of the Hat Creek Rim Overlook sign.

The Hat Creek Rim is a 1000-foot ridge that invites all sorts of outdoor enthusiasts to play—from dog walkers and hikers, to mountain bikers and even hang-gliding enthusiasts. It's not unusual to see multicolored gliders floating on the thermals created when wind sweeps up the valley all summer. Indeed, the rim hosts a large hang-gliding event every Labor Day.

While this hike is a blast in the spring, summer, and fall, winter is the time the girls love this jaunt the most. And so will you. If you've never tried snowshoeing, this is just the trip to learn. You'll travel through a volcanic world that is softened by snow, and the terrain is flat and the path is wide. Unlike cross-country or downhill skiing, where there is a learning curve to good performance, the basics of snowshoeing have never changed. If you can walk, you can snowshoe.

Snowshoeing is gaining in popularity, and it's considered the fastest-growing of all winter sports. Compared to other winter activities, snowshoeing ranks as one of the easiest to enjoy—and one of the best winter fitness regimes. Hiking uphill in unpacked snow can easily burn

One-way trip to Baker Lake

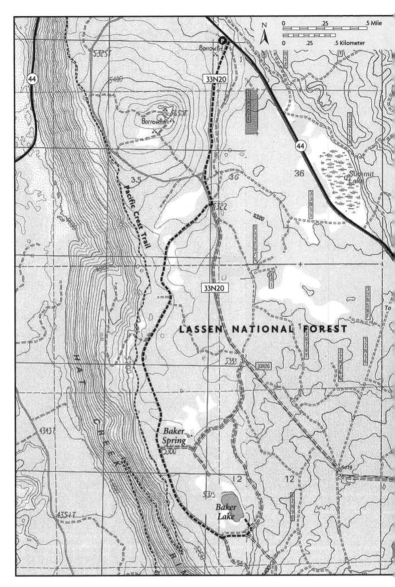

1000 calories an hour, according to fitness experts.

The tone of this hike, though, is ease. It starts on cinder-covered FR 33N20. Ignore the branch roads until you get to an obvious branch at 1.2 miles, where you'll start climbing up signed FR 33N20A. This is the route you'll stay on all the way to Baker Lake, probably snow covered in winter since this is a shallow wisp of a waterway.

Because of a devastating forest fire more than 10 years ago, you'll march through a forest of Jeffrey pine that's uniform in size. The forest was planted after the fire; you can see the blaze's full power on display from Hat Creek Rim.

After a slight downhill at 1.6 miles, look for open views of Prospect Peak to the south. Then, when you come to an open view of the rim at about 3 miles, hike some 75 yards to one of the most spectacular views of Lassen Peak, especially striking when decked out in its winter cloak. This is a postcard-worthy picture; make sure you bring your camera.

I usually get to Baker Lake, at 3.5 miles in, have a snack, cook up some hot chocolate, and let the girls gnaw on a rawhide chewy before backtracking back to the truck. You can turn around any time you like.

19. Crystal and Baum Lakes

Round trip: 5 miles
Hiking time: 3 hours
High point: 3000 feet
Elevation gain: 100 feet
Best hiking time: Year-round; snow possible in winter
Water: From Baum and Crystal Lakes
Map: USGS Cassel
Contact: Pacific Gas and Electric Co., 1 (800) 743-5000 or *www.pge.com*

Getting there: From Redding, take Highway 299 east to the intersection of Highways 299 and 89, about 54 miles from Interstate 5. From the intersection, drive another 2 miles on Highway 299 and turn south onto the paved Cassel Road. Go 2 more miles and turn left at the sign for the state-run Crystal Lake Fish Hatchery. Drive another mile and turn left into the paved parking lot of Baum Lake.

On a good day, my dogs will let me fish after hiking for a good hour, but those days are few and far between. While Scully will plop down and watch the world go by, Trinity is unwilling to afford me that luxury often. She's constantly getting in the water, swimming, jumping, and making sure I see

Round trip to Crystal and Baum Lakes

Crystal and Baum Lakes offer fishing and great solitude.

her. Crystal and Baum Lakes are full of fish—German brown, brook, and rainbow trout. Big ones, up to 20 pounds, along with planted fish that are just right for the grill, at a half pound each.

And while I do get to fish once and again, I always enjoy going back to these lakes for the hike it affords the girls and me. I manage to see something different each time out. The lakes offer a peace that is hard to find these days. Osprey and hawks circle overhead (there's always a chance to watch the osprey hunt, grabbing a fish from the lake and turning it so it faces forward to be more aerodynamic), while all manner of shorebirds and waterfowl squawk, chirp, whistle, and honk.

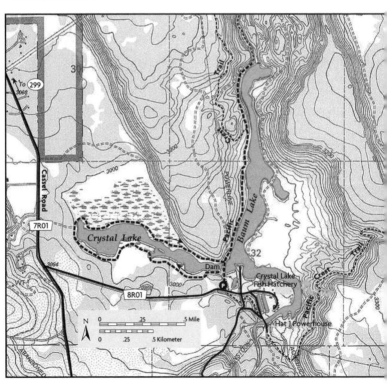

The trail network traces the shoreline of both lakes and is used by anglers and hikers alike. Start from the parking lot and take the path that leads to a dam that separates the two lakes. Cross the dam to the north side and then head left for the path that follows Crystal Lake's shoreline. It's an easy hike around the lake, where you'll likely to see white pelicans bobbing on the water during their migration inland. You'll pass grasslands and low brush, like squawbrush, sage, and western juniper. You'll loop around to your starting point at a grove of ponderosa pine; look north for a great view of Mount Shasta.

Your other choice from the north side of the dam is the 1.5-mile path along Baum Lake's western shoreline, where you'll link up with the Pacific Crest Trail. Follow the trail north—it's obvious—where you'll soon get to a split in the trail. The upper fork goes up a slope, crosses a fence, and reaches another fork. The PCT heads left and uphill from the midslope trail, but you can stay right and you'll reach the lower trail, which never leaves the shore.

You can continue along this path to the Baum Lake Dam, and continue on to the Hat Creek 2 Powerhouse, or just retrace your steps to the dam separating Baum and Crystal Lakes, where you might snatch a few minutes to cast a line for dinner.

20. Hat Creek Trail

Round trip: 8.6 miles
Hiking time: 5 hours
High point: 4300 feet
Elevation gain: 400 feet
Best hiking time: Year-round
Water: From Hat Creek
Map: USGS Old Station
Contact: Lassen National Forest, Hat Creek Ranger District, (530) 336-5521

Getting there: From the junctions of Highways 44 and 89 near Old Station, turn north onto Highway 89 and drive 0.3 mile and turn left into Cave Campground. Go 30 yards and park in the small lot to the left.

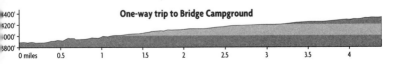

Hat Creek Valley under a canopy of clouds.

From late April through mid-November, this trail is teeming with anglers, sniffing out the best places to chase the thousands of rainbow and brook trout the California Department of Fish and Game plants each general trout fishing season.

Oh, you'll see others on the trail, retired folks walking hand-in-hand as they take a break from their recreational vehicle wanderings, teens heading to secret swimming holes, and certainly, dog walkers—and happy dogs who rush from the trail to Hat Creek for a dip or drink. The rushing waters of spring-fed Hat Creek and the canopy of riparian forest bring trekkers here all year, from the crunch of fall leaves, through the crunch of snow in winter and the renewed energy of spring, all the way through the heat of another Northern California summer.

From the parking area, cross the wooden bridge over Hat Creek and pick up the trail on the right. Just a 0.5 mile from the bridge, you'll get to a concrete bridge and gorge that shows off the power of this little stream. A narrow slot has been cut through the porous lava rock, where mini waterfalls crash through the channel, until the stream slowly widens. The wide, sandy trail never leaves Hat Creek for more than a few yards, since, after all, it's a fishing access trail.

At 1 mile, you'll come across a grove of white-trunked aspens, which are rich green in summer and turn golden in fall. You'll also notice the mix of huge ponderosa pine and incense cedar, species that aren't so water-friendly, mixing with water-loving species like alder and willow. There's even live oak and, off the trail, a maze of chaparral shrubs like bitterbrush, mountain mahogany, greenleaf manzanita, western juniper, California sage, and rabbit goldenweed mixed in for good measure.

In the spring and summer, you'll find black-tailed deer here, also songbirds, Steller's jays loudly begging for a dropped crumb, osprey, and the occasional eagle. I've heard of people spotting bobcat, but I have never seen one of these elusive cats here.

While the trail is shrouded mostly by the riparian forest, there are views

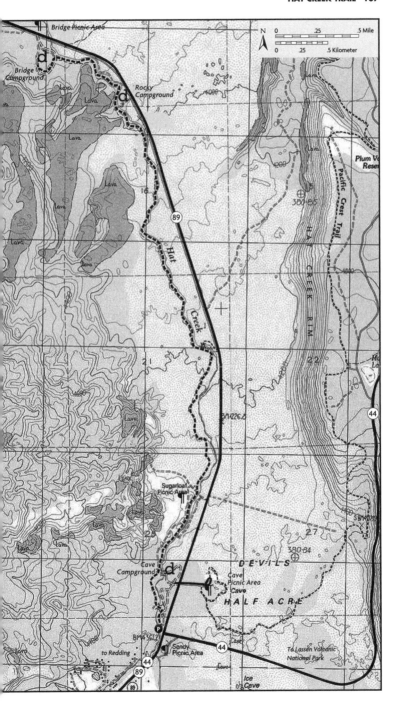

of the surrounding volcano-enhanced landscape. Lassen Peak, ghostly white in winter, is prominent on the return trip to your car. But also look for Sugarloaf Peak, Hat Creek Rim (in summer, hang gliders use the rim as a take-off point), Freaner Peak, and Burney Mountain.

At 1.8 miles, you'll reach another stand of aspen, then another waterfall a short time later. At 2.2 miles, you're treated to a second waterfall, while entering a strip of conifer forest of white fir and sugar pine. Walk another 0.25 mile and you'll come across a third waterfall. The scene is repeated at 2.7 miles.

At 3 miles, you'll be treated to views of Magee and Crater Peaks toward the west, from another stand of aspen. The trail leads to another wooden bridge, announcing Rocky Campground at 3.8 miles. Traverse the basalt talus here, where you actually look down on Hat Creek, then continue on to Bridge Campground at 4.3 miles and the terminus of the trail. You could opt to use a car shuttle for a one-way option, or turn around and go back the way you came.

21. Caribou Wilderness Area

Round trip: 6.8 miles
Hiking time: 5 hours or overnight
High point: 7100 feet
Elevation gain: 600 feet
Best hiking time: Fall; hikable year-round, be prepared for swarms of mosquitoes in spring
Water: From lakes
Map: USGS Bogard Buttes
Contact: Lassen National Forest, Almanor Ranger District, (530) 295-4251

Getting there: You can access this area from the south via Highway 36 or from the north via Highway 44. From the south, take Highway 36 to Chester and turn left on Forest Road 10. Follow the road to a left turn on FR 30N25 and follow that a short distance to the Indian Meadow parking area. From

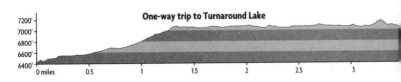

The relative flatness of the Caribou Wilderness makes it a good choice for families with children.

here, all of the southern Caribou lakes are accessible. From the north, take Highway 44 toward Susanville. Just past the Bogard Work Center is the right turn on FR 10. Take a left on FR 32N09 and follow it to the Cone Lake parking lot and trailhead. The hike description below leaves from Cone Lake.

Fall is the best time of year for hardy souls to make those final backpacking trips before the blanket of winter tucks everything up in white—and the Caribou Wilderness Area on the backside of Lassen Volcanic National Park is probably my most-favorite camping destination with the girls.

Backpackers might need to get out their silk sleeping-bag liners for a bit of extra warmth, but the prospect of a few last weekends in the woods is alive and well. You can sense it in the valley: people who love to sleep with the windows open in Redding are getting up in the middle of the night to get out an extra comforter; condensation covers car windows. And in the mountains? Frost has already settled into some valleys. You can see your breath as you light the stove for that must-have cup of coffee after slipping from your cocoon of bag and tent.

In the fall, you just might be the only overnight guest in the whole 20,500-acre wilderness that's all of 9 miles long and 5 miles wide. The entire wilderness sits at about 6900 feet along a rolling volcanic plateau, so the hiking is easy. In fact, the highest point in the entire wilderness is the 8374-foot Red Cinder, a peak that straddles the wilderness and Lassen Volcanic National Park.

Sure, there's a bit more gear to lug on a fall hike—it's really the only time that I actually take a tent and there's that extra fleece clothing. But to sit out at dusk in front of a warming fire and let all the stress of uncertain times melt away is priceless. And finding a lake to call your very own should be a cinch in the fall. The wilderness is filled with lake options,

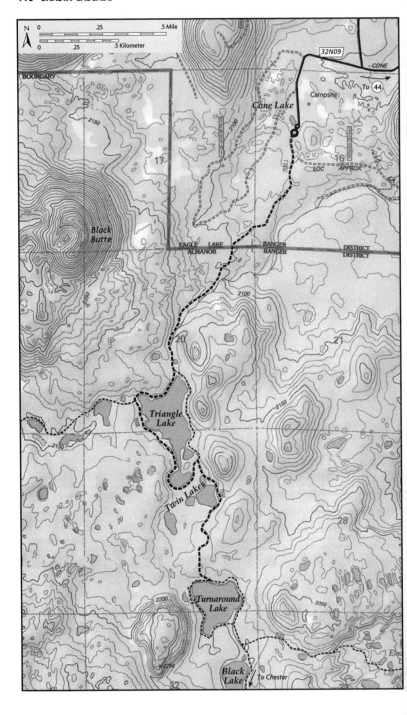

most of which sustain a population of rainbow and German brown trout.

The last fall trek I took in the wilderness was probably one of the most fulfilling trips I've ever taken. Starting on the trailhead from the north, the dogs and I hit Triangle Lake, about 1.8 miles in and one of the largest lakes in the wilderness, in about 15 minutes. I took a short rest to watch the waves ripple across the surface while Scully and Trinity busied themselves log hopping near the shore.

We continued 1.6 more miles to Turnaround Lake and settled into one of the best lakeside campsites to be found anywhere. The site sits under the cover of lodgepole pine, with a small fire ring that's positioned right near a granite knob. The lake panorama is punctuated by a large granite point with a lone lodgepole pine, the perfect place to drag a dry fly behind a plastic bubble to entice trout that are cruising the shoreline for a meal.

By nightfall, the steam was rising from the lake, a few snowflakes floated from the sky, and the dogs' breath came out in white bursts. By 9:00 p.m., I was ready to scrunch into my sleeping bag and zone out for several hours. When I awoke, I was greeted by a 2-inch layer of snow. Everything was crystallized in white. Truly magical.

22. McGowan Lake Trail

Round trip: 4.4 miles
Hiking time: 3–5 hours
High point: 6500 feet
Elevation gain: 500 feet
Best hiking time: Winter; hikable year-round
Water: Bring your own
Map: USGS Lassen Peak
Contact: Lassen National Forest, Almanor Ranger District, (530) 295-4251

Getting there: From the town of Red Bluff, take Highway 36 to the signed Morgan Summit at the junction of Highway 36 and the Lassen

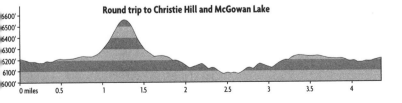

Round trip to Christie Hill and McGowan Lake

Park Highway, just east of the town of Mineral and northwest of the town of Chester. Turn north onto the Lassen Park Highway, go 2 miles, and park at the free clearing where a snow-covered Forest Service road (your trail) is located.

You've never tried snowshoeing with your dog? Here's your chance to finally get out on snowshoes—it's easy—and have some winter fun with the dogs.

This is a peaceful route that takes you deep into a dark and snow-covered forest, though with several clearings for long-distance views to the south. You'll also see huge rock outcroppings and the swift-flowing Nanny Creek, where there's the chance for a snow picnic.

Even in the nearly quiet winter months, this trail allows for great wildlife viewing. Coyote have been seen making their way along the creek for a drink, or to ambush the

Along the route to Nanny Creek: McGowan Lake (photo by Marc Soares)

snowshoe hare and mice that venture out from time to time. You might get to see a porcupine or great horned owl in the trunks of the conifers, while the chirps of mountain chickadees and the screech of Steller's jays punctuate the normal silence.

Since you'll be walking on a wide Forest Service road, you'll likely be sharing the trek with cross-country skiers, especially after a big snowstorm blows through. Because of the elevation, the snow falls airy and light—and it tends to get piled on everything in site.

From the parking area, you'll drop a bit, then begin to climb into a lodgepole pine forest, which then leads to a dense white-fir forest. At just over a mile, you'll swing around a manzanita-covered hillside (you might see snowshoe hare scatter into the cover of dense brush) and you'll catch a great view of Brokeoff Mountain to the north, inside Lassen Volcanic

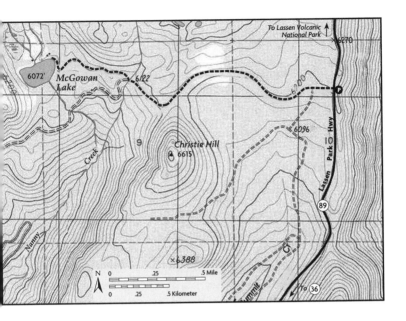

National Park (where, sadly, dogs are not allowed on the trails).

From here, you can climb nearby Christie Hill (6559 feet) to the south. It can be reached from its eastern flanks, then by picking your way safely through the white-fir forest to the crest of the hill. To get the best views of Lassen Peak, you'll need to wend your way through the conifers.

Not into the adventure of climbing a peak in the middle of winter? Stay the course and you'll get to the creek, which is swift and free-flowing from the blockade of several giant volcanic boulders. From here, you descend through incense cedar and Jeffrey pine (the cones won't prick your hands when you run them over the surface, unlike the cones of a ponderosa pine, where the burrs stick sharply out), and the forest opens up. You'll reach Nanny Creek at 1.7 miles, where you can watch the frothy water tumble over snowcapped boulders.

Don't miss going just 0.3 mile farther, where you'll come to an area of multitrunked cedars in a giant boulder outcropping near McGowan Lake, which is 0.2 mile farther on. From this vantage point, you'll get great views of the Cascade Range to the north and the Sierra Nevada to the south. The outcropping also makes a great place to get out of the elements, enjoy a snack (and maybe some hot chocolate, if so equipped), and rest before returning from whence you came.

23. Lake Almanor Recreation Trail

Round trip: Up to 19 miles
Hiking time: 3–7 hours
High point: 4600 feet
Elevation gain: 300 feet
Best hiking time: Year-round; a great snowshoe route
Water: Bring your own
Map: Lassen National Forest
Contact: Lassen National Forest, Almanor Ranger District, (530) 295-4251

Getting there: From Redding, take Interstate 5 south 35 miles to Red Bluff and take the Highway 36 exit. Turn left onto Highway 36 and follow it through town, taking another left at the split junction of Highways 36 and 99. It's another 78 miles to the intersection of Highways 36 and 89 near the town of Chester. At the intersection, take Highway 89 south 4.6 miles to a plowed (in winter) parking area across from the Humbug Road turnoff.

In summer, the Lake Almanor Recreation Trail is a wide, inviting paved path that meanders along the scenic western shore of this lake, which has 55 miles of shoreline and is 13 miles long and 6 miles wide. The lake was created in 1914 to fuel a hydroelectric plant operated by the Great Western Power Company; its name is a combination of Alice, Martha, and Elinore, the daughters of the company's vice president. Canyon Dam, on the lakeshore, was built in 1927 to harness the North Fork Feather River.

Great Western Power was later bought by Puget Gas and Electric who, along with the Forest Service, developed this area into the four-season recreation spot it is today. Indeed, you'll find a mix of PG&E and Forest Service campgrounds along the recreation trail, which in the summer is popular with anglers, cyclists, roller bladers, picnickers (picnic tables and

One-way trip to east end of trail

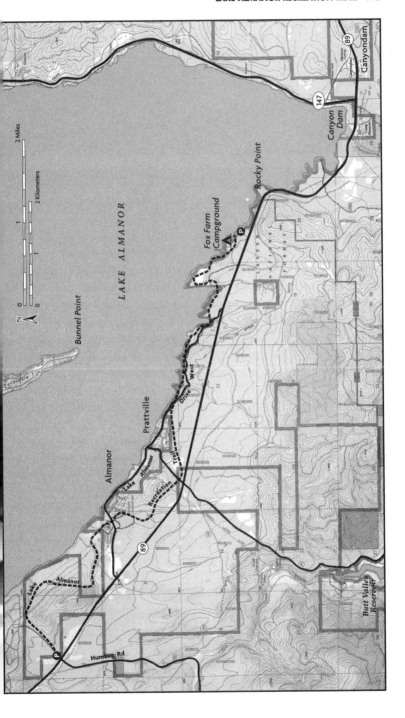

The Lake Almanor Recreation Trail shouldn't be missed on snowshoes.

benches dot the entire length of the trail), and dog walkers.

But not in winter. It's at this time that the trail takes on a look of mystery, and a sense of adventure. Be sure to bring a fishing rod, since the rainbow and German brown trout fishing is best from November through May, with anglers reportedly catching 4- to 6-pound fish right from the rocky shoreline. Listen for wildlife as well, although much of it departs the winter chill for warmer climes. Still, you'll see and hear plenty of waterfowl as well as shorebirds: the shrill sound of plovers, the chirping of chickadees, the caw of ravens, and the screeches of Steller's jays. Always keep an eye trained for the osprey and bald eagles that hunt for fish in the winter. Or at least, watch the folly as an osprey swoops from on high to take a trout from the chilly water—only to be chased and robbed by a bald eagle. Both species are prevalent on this lake.

But the amount of snowbound adventure and wildlife you take in is up to you: although the trail is 9.5 miles long, it's up to you to decide when to turn back.

The trail starts 75 yards from the parking area. After a mile of trudging through powdery snow in the shadow of a ponderosa-pine forest and the occasional huge white pine, the trail offers up a glimpse of its magic. Even with 6 feet of snow built up around the lake, you'll recognize that you've entered a series of meadows that dot the path. Looking west, you'll see the Almanor Peninsula and behind that, the white-capped peaks of Little Dyer and Dyer Mountain (which is rumored to be the location of a new, four-season resort that will rival those near Lake Tahoe).

After about a mile, the trail follows the shoreline closely before heading inland again toward the Plumas Pines Resort. It then skirts the Old Prattville Cemetery, crosses Almanor Drive West (watch for traffic), and then again follows the shoreline toward an array of campgrounds (which are closed in winter).

Choose your own turnaround point. You'll find several snow-covered coves that are inviting, with squawking geese—and swooping osprey.

24. Bizz Johnson Trail

Round trip: 13 miles
Hiking time: 7 hours or overnight
High point: 4660 feet
Elevation gain: 500 feet
Best hiking time: Year-round
Water: From Boulder Creek
Maps: USGS Susanville, USGS Roop Mountain
Contact: Bureau of Land Management, Eagle Lake Resource Area,
(530) 257-0456; Lassen National Forest, Susanville Ranger District,
(530) 257-2151

Getting there: From Redding, take Highway 44/89 about 110 miles to Susanville. To get to the depot, take Highway 36 to Susanville and turn south on Weatherlow Street, which soon becomes Richmond Road. After 0.5 mile, park for free across from the depot. Signs will point you to the trail.

This is the way to run a railroad, albeit an abandoned one. The Bizz Johnson Trail links Susanville and the community of Westwood and is a 25-mile multiuse route that follows the rugged Susan River canyon. The trail is a combined effort between the Lassen Land and Trails Trust, the Bureau of Land Management, the Forest Service, and the Rails to Trails Conservancy (a Washington DC–based advocacy group that helps buy old rail right-of-ways).

The historic trail actually is the former right-of-way of the Fernley and Lassen Railroad, built in 1914 to connect a logging mill in Westwood to the railroad's mail line in Fernley, Nevada. The line operated for more than forty years, first run by Fernley and Lassen and later by Central Pacific and Southern Pacific Rail Corporation.

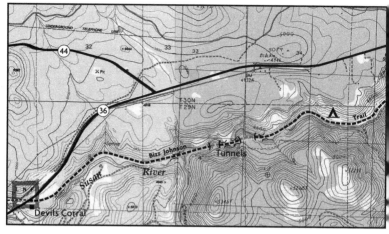

This hike covers the eastern portion of the trail, from the Susanville Railroad Depot to Devils Corral off Highway 36, some 6.5 miles away. You certainly could use a car shuttle, or go out and back, or even consider spending the night. Rules include no camping within a mile of a trailhead or near the south side of the road west of Hobo Camp, which is right outside of Susanville. Camping on BLM land is limited to 3 days; you can stay 14 days in Lassen National Forest.

In summer, the Susan River is a great place to fish for rainbow trout or to enjoy a quick dip in waters that are quite refreshing. From mid-October through mid-November, the trail comes alive with the golden hues of the cottonwoods and the reds and oranges of the scattered oaks. The Rails to Trails Conservancy named the Bizz Johnson one of the eight best trails to catch fall foliage shows in the United States. When winter sets in, there's no need to abandon this trail. Pack the booties, strap on snowshoes, and glide along, watching for deer, rabbit, and raccoon tracks in the snow.

The trail is dog- and family-friendly, wide with a gentle slope toward Westwood. The grade rarely exceeds 3 percent along the entire 25.6-mile length.

Start off the first mile with a gentle jaunt through a couple of neighborhoods, before coming to a metal bridge that crosses a great first swimming hole. It's here where you'll see the stark contrast between the dry, sheer rock faces of the Susan River canyon and the lushness of the riparian habitat. You'll cross a small wooden bridge at 1.5 miles that overlooks the gravel bars of the Susan River, where in the summer you'll find the locals swimming, inner tubing, and fishing for rainbow trout.

At just over 2 miles, the former rail line trail reaches a well-placed bench and several spur trails that lead to the water's edge. Many walkers choose

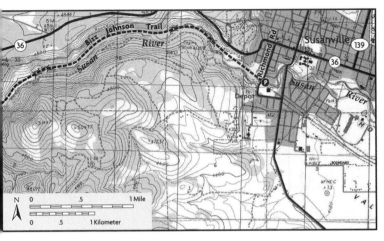

to rest and turn back here, and you'll notice if you press on that you just might have the rest of the trek to yourself. From this point as well, you'll get into the pristine forest views and wild stretches of river.

The girls and I never (well, never in the summer) miss perhaps the largest and deepest swimming hole along the entire trail at 2.8 miles. It can be found just below a concrete and wood bridge. A mile farther, you'll find a nice campsite on the far shore.

After following the Susan River at its level, past the campsite, you'll start to rise well above the rushing water. Cross another bridge at 4.8 miles, then spend some time taking in one of the most interesting features of this trek—an old railroad tunnel that stays chilly right through the 100-degree heat

of summer. Rail workers used explosives to cut this 150-yard tunnel through the solid cliff face in 1914.

The next 1.5 miles to Devils Corral features more of the same: sheer cliff walls; a wide, inviting path; cool swimming and fishing holes; and slender, long strips of tall grasses along the water's edge. Be sure not to miss this trek in winter, when the scenes are softened by a blanket of snow.

Bridge over the Susan River (photo by Marc Soares)

SACRAMENTO AND THE GOLD COUNTRY

25. South Yuba Independence Trail

Round trip: 7 Miles
Hiking time: 3 hours
High point: 1450 feet
Elevation gain: negligible
Best hiking time: Year-round
Water: Bring your own
Map: USGS Nevada City
Contact: South Yuba River State Park, Bridgeport Visitor Center and Ranger Station, (530) 432-2546

Getting there: From Nevada City, drive 5.5 miles north on Highway 49 and park in turnouts near the trailhead, which is about 0.5 mile south of the Yuba River Bridge. If you reach the bridge, you've gone too far. Be careful walking across Highway 49.

The mid-1850s in gold rush crazy Nevada County brought engineering marvels of all kinds to extract the precious metal from the streambeds

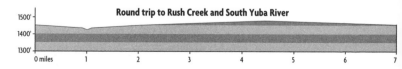

Round trip to Rush Creek and South Yuba River

North Fork of the American River (photo by Marc Soares)

and canyon walls. The origin of the Independence Trail was an old miner's ditch once known at the Excelsior Canal. It was built in 1859 to carry water from the South Yuba River to hydraulic mining sites in Smartville, some 25 miles away. California legislators outlawed hydraulic mining in 1885, and until 1967 the canal was used for irrigation.

According to the nonprofit hiking group Sequoya Challenge, Oakland Museum docent John Olmstead rediscovered the entire water system in 1975. And what a system. First, there was the ditch, which carried the water; then there was the berm, where the ditch-tender treaded to check the system and all the wooden flumes that bridged the ravines. Olmstead's wish was to answer a friend's lifelong dream: "Please find me a level wilderness trail where I can reach out and touch the wildflowers from my wheelchair."

Don't think you can walk your dogs in a wilderness setting? This is the hike for you. The trail is gloriously flat, a fantastic walk that takes you though history. It rests inside South Yuba River State Park and is the very first wilderness trail in the country designed to be wheelchair accessible,

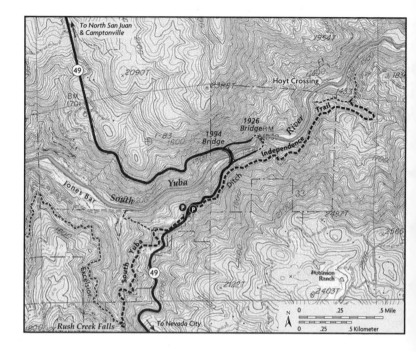

according to Sequoya Challenge. The entire wheelchair loop is 7 miles.

Your car is parked midway along this trail, which runs west and east. Going west along the unmaintained portion, you'll find a fantastic waterfall just a mile from the trailhead. People and wheelchairs then can travel a switchback ramp from Flume 28 (520-feet long) to the sparkling waters of Rush Creek.

As you stroll along the western trail, you'll come upon a grand overlook of the South Yuba River. In spring, the overlook is covered in wildflowers. Come summer, the canyons switch to green, then dress up for autumn in red and gold hues.

Hike back and take a stroll along the eastern trail. You'll cross cliff-hanging flumes, take in more great views of the river and surrounding foothills, and have the opportunity to take a dip in several swimming holes that have been scooped out of the granite. The eastern side of the route is 2.5 miles of maintained trail.

Along the entire trail, you'll find picnic areas, restrooms, and even a camping area designed for disabled guests. This truly is a trail for all people—and their dogs, too. Sequoya Challenge offers guided hikes for a small donation; call (530) 477-4788.

26. Bullards Bar Trail

Round trip: 14 miles
Hiking time: 7 hours
High point: 2243 feet
Elevation gain: negligible
Best hiking time: Spring; hikable year-round
Water: From reservoir; or bring your own
Maps: USGS Camptonville, USGS Challenge
Contact: Tahoe National Forest, North Yuba Ranger Station, (530) 288-3231

Getting there: From Nevada City, take Highway 49 North to Marysville Road (2 miles south of Camptonville) and turn left. Follow Marysville Road for 2.6 miles to the Dark Day turnoff. Turn right and drive down to the parking area above the boat ramp. Both the east and west trail sections can be accessed from here.

Dogs that like to swim will love the Bullards Bar Trail. Owners who like to swim, fish, and view wildflowers will love it just as much.

This easy trail follows the contours of Bullards Bar Reservoir, a 4700-acre lake that offers 56 miles of shoreline wrapped by both the Plumas and Tahoe National Forests. Most people hike this trail in spring, when temperatures are most comfortable, but don't forget that as the summer wears on, use drops. One of the best features of this recreation area is that it's heavily wooded with huge ponderosa pine and Douglas fir, which means every campground site is shaded from the heat of a Sierra Nevada foothills summer. With the lake within easy distance for the entire 14-mile trip, there's always the chance to cool off. And you'll always get the feeling that you're the only one at this clear mountain lake, which doesn't get as much pressure as some other Northern California reservoirs.

But spring is prime here. During a spring storm, the dogs and I never had a raindrop touch us because of the dense forest covering. The underbrush is ripe with wildflowers and giant ferns, which thrive under the canopy.

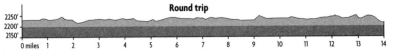

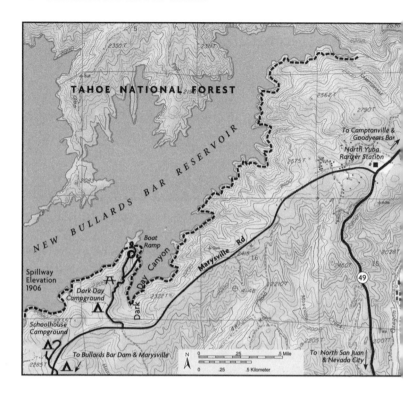

This hike starts at the Dark Day Campground, where you have the option to go east or west. You can also link up with the 23 other miles of trail in and around the recreation area, including Schoolhouse, 8-Ball, 7-Ball, and Rebel Ridge.

Don't be daunted by the 14-mile distance (if you do both sections). This in an uncomplicated trek with plenty of options. The trail is flat, wide, and inviting and always offers a great lake view. Most people take off east or west, dink and dunk in the water, stop at the vista point above the dam for the view, and maybe drop a line before heading back to the car. There's no hassle here, no pressure. Relax.

Lupine grows in abundance near Bullards Bar Reservoir.

27. Codfish Creek Trail

Round trip: 3.4 miles
Hiking time: 2 hours
High point: 950 feet
Elevation gain: 110 feet
Best hiking time: Spring through fall
Water: Best to bring your own
Map: USGS Colfax
Contact: Auburn State Recreation Area, (916) 885-4527

Getting there: The trailhead is on Ponderosa Way, 6 miles south of the town of Weimar. From Auburn, take Interstate 80 east to the second Weimar exit (Weimar Cross Roads) and turn right on Canyon Way. After about a mile, the road turns left and becomes Ponderosa Way. Drive to the parking area, on the right just before the bridge over the North Fork American River. The trailhead is beyond parking area. Note: Ponderosa Way is a rough road, made for high-clearance and four-wheel-drive vehicles. It can get treacherous in winter.

Granted, the Codfish Creek Trail takes a bit to get to, but the views are worth the trip. It's an easy trail, gaining just over 100 feet in a little more than 3 miles. In the springtime—the best time to go, really—the trail comes alive with several species of wildflowers and butterflies, which are attracted to flowers' sweet nectar. And of course, the terminus of this hike is a spectacular, 40-foot waterfall, which usually dries up in the summer.

An excellent brochure detailing the area's flora and fauna is available at a discovery marker located 0.25 mile from the trailhead across the sandy beach. The pamphlet was written and illustrated by Heather K. Mehl for her 2001 senior project at Colfax High School, according to the good folks at the Auburn State Recreation Area.

The trail begins at the north side of the bridge on Ponderosa Way and leads downstream on the sunny, exposed side of the canyon, following an old mining route along the North Fork American River. The river was mined extensively for gold well into the twentieth century. Along the trail, you'll be

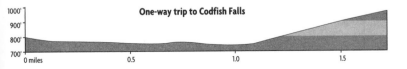

One-way trip to Codfish Falls

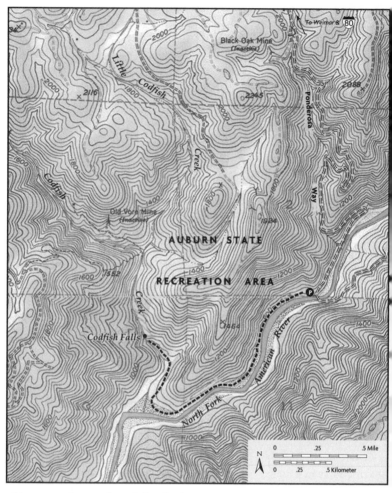

able to see the results of the dredge-mining operations: just look for the large, uniform piles of river cobble on the opposite side of the river.

The first mile is relatively flat, and there are plenty of side trails that lead to the water's edge so the dogs can catch a dip and a drink. While at the river's edge, look for dippers (water ouzels)—a small, brownish-gray bird about the size of a robin, searching out a meal. They bob up and down, then dive suddenly below the water's surface. Mergansers—waterfowl that hunt fish—are also prevalent here. In spring, the males will be wearing their brilliant mating colors, then will transform in summer to a color closer to the female.

This is also a classic trail to view the riparian habitat. Three species of oak can be found here, including canyon live oak, black oak, and interior live oak. You'll also find Pacific madrone and manzanita, which are sometimes mistaken for each other since they both have smooth, reddish-brown trunks. Known as one of the more exotic of the western hardwoods, Pacific madrone is distinguished by a very consistent salmon color, beautiful knot patterns, and a smooth grain. The wood is prized for exotic flooring, furniture, cabinetry, and picture frames, according to a woodworking craftsman I know. You'll also be treated to huge stands of

Gray pine at North Fork American River, early fall (photo by Marc Soares)

ponderosa pine, grey pine (also known at foothill pine), and Douglas fir.

At 1.2 miles, you'll catch the turn for Codfish Creek and the falls. The trail cuts up to the right through the Codfish Creek canyon to the falls, a mere 0.5 mile away from the turnoff.

28. American River Parkway

One-way: Up to 23 miles
Hiking time: 0.5 hour to all day
High point: 500 feet
Elevation gain: 300 feet
Best hiking time: Spring and fall; hikable year-round
Water: Along the trail from potable-water taps; or bring your own
Maps: USGS Sacramento East, USGS Carmichael, USGS Citrus Heights, USGS Folsom
Contact: County of Sacramento, Parks and Recreation Division, (916) 875-6961

Getting there: The trail begins at Discovery Park in Old Sacramento, on the north side of the American River. From Interstate 5, take the Richards

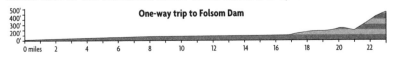

Oaks along the American River Parkway

Boulevard exit and drive west to Jiboom Street. Turn right and follow the road to the park. There are other access points along US 50 as well. Each county park along the trail charges $4 a car to park, although no permit is required to hike. The Folsom Lake State Recreation Area charges $3 per car.

Every city, it seems, has a trail where dog walkers can see and be seen. In Sacramento, that trail is the American River Parkway, a 23-mile (one-way) paved trail that links Sacramento with the towns of Rancho Cordova, Fair Oaks, and Folsom. There are actually two parallel trails happening here. One is the paved American River Parkway for cyclists and roller bladers, then there's the dirt Jedediah Smith Memorial Trail for horses, trail runners, and hikers.

Certainly no one does the entire trip in one fell swoop; people tend to enjoy short sections and return to their cars to continue with their busy lives. Evening seems to be the busiest time along the trail, when its crowded with joggers and dog walkers.

The trail is a year-round destination, but spring and fall tend to be the best times for out-of-towners to visit. In spring, the grass and trees along the river are richly green, the water is flowing fresh and clear, and you'll have the chance to see American shad—in huge schools— complete their migration from the ocean into the river to spawn. This fish is revered by anglers, since it packs a punch when caught on light

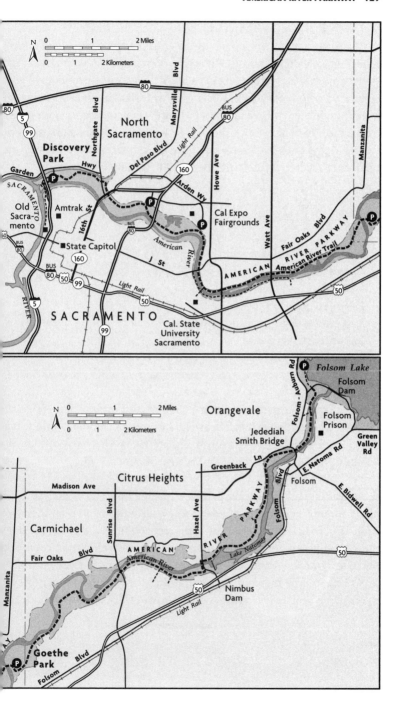

tackle. In fall, the trees burst into reds, golds and oranges.

The trail gets some 5 million visitors a year, so if you're looking for solitude, this isn't a trail for you. But it is a good hike to get your dogs socialized to group settings that include a lot of dogs. Remember to have good control of your pet, since not everyone will share in your dog's exuberance to meet new people and dogs. It's the perfect place to work on the command, "leave it," which most dog handlers teach for good behavior.

The American River Parkway is even a movie star, of sorts. The trail was used as a backdrop in the Kurt Russell 1997 thriller *Breakdown*.

29. Summit Lake Trail

Round trip: 4 miles
Hiking time: 2 hours
High point: 7400 feet
Elevation gain: 200 feet
Best hiking time: June through October
Water: Bring your own
Map: USGS Norden
Contact: Tahoe National Forest, Truckee Ranger District, (530) 587-3558

Getting there: From Auburn, drive 60 miles east on Interstate 80 to the Castle Peak Area/Boreal Ridge Road exit just west of Donner Summit. Take the exit, turn right, then turn immediately left. Drive 0.4 mile to the trailhead for Donner Summit and the Pacific Crest Trail.

A buddy of mine, a dog lover and travel writer, asked if I was going to include Summit Lake in this guidebook. I hadn't thought about it, since I really don't often get to this part of the state on my jaunts with the dogs.

"Oh, you have to include Summit Lake," he said. "I don't know of any dog from San Francisco or Sacramento that hasn't used this trail."

So I did a little research, and found that the trail is canine-approved by *www.dogfriendly.com*, a website that provides city and travel guides for

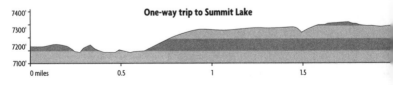

One-way trip to Summit Lake

people and their pets. Next thing was to take a trip out I-80 to Donner Summit and the Summit Lake Trail.

OK, it's not much of a trail for some people, but it is a scenic trip that can be done—out-and-back—in just a couple of hours. And even in late fall, when the weather was crisp and there was the threat of snow in the air, carloads of people were streaming off I-80 to stretch their legs and let their dogs stretch too.

Dogs should be on a leash unless they behave when off-leash and are under direct voice command. Normally my border collie cross Trinity is great at voice commands—until she gets into the middle of a pack of dogs. We stayed leashed the entire 4-mile round trip.

The first mile of the hike follows the wide and inviting PCT in an easterly direction, then picks its way north for another mile, passing through a tunnel under I-80. Just after emerging from the tunnel, you'll see the intersection with the Summit Lake Trail. This is where you'll gain

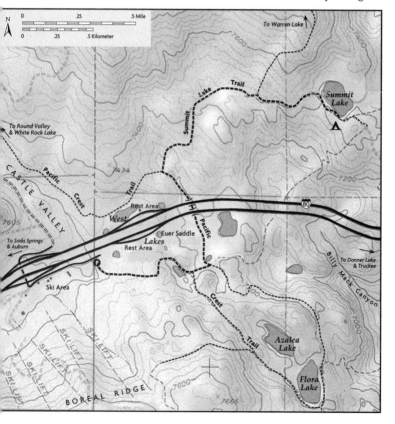

almost all of your elevation.

You'll cross two small creeks, which are separated by a low, glaciated granite ridge. The trail then bends through a meadow that's ablaze with wildflowers in the spring and early summer. The trail continues past the intersection with the signed trail for Warren Lake, where you'll want to veer right and out to the edge of a ridge. From here, it's a short walk under a canopy of pine to the southern corner of the Summit Lake.

Dogs love romping on the Summit Lake Trail.

Camping is available here, but most people sit a bit and head back to the car. Don't forget to pack a light fishing rod, since the lake is full of brook and rainbow trout. If you're fishing, don't forget that your California Department of Fish and Game license must be visible on your person anywhere from the waist up.

30. Folsom Lake and Mormon Island Dam

Round trip: 13 miles
Hiking time: 6 hours or overnight
High point: 600 feet
Elevation gain: 400 feet
Best hiking time: Early spring; hikable year-round
Water: From the Folsom Lake
Map: USGS Folsom
Contact: Folsom Lake Recreation Area, (916) 988-0205

Getting there: From US 50 in Sacramento, take Folsom Boulevard north for 2.8 miles. Turn right on East Natoma Street and drive 3.1 miles. Turn

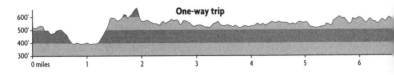

right on the paved road signed for Folsom Point. Drive another 0.7 mile and turn left to the picnic area and beach.

When the summer sun is high in the sky and everyone from Sacramento, it seems, has escaped the valley heat with their boats and personal watercraft, this is a trail best avoided by dogs and their owners. Just too much saturation.

But in the months before and after the high season (May through September), this lake is ideal for a stroll with the dogs, since it offers 75 miles of shoreline. On some weekends in the early spring, late fall, and winter, you'll think you own the lake, since you might not see another person for miles. Your only company, besides your trusted canine companion, will be the American kestrels, red-tailed hawks, and eagles that soar on the

Folsom Lake, early spring (photo by Marc Soares)

thermals; the honking of Canada geese; and, if you're lucky, a bobcat or raccoon at sunset coming down to the lake for a drink or a meal.

Starting at the picnic area and beach—after a long car ride, what dog doesn't like a refreshing dip?—the trail winds its way past a small cove that's full of willows. You'll continue across Mormon Island Dam and the 1-mile Dike 8 Trail, where you'll get a great view of the entire 18,000-acre lake. To the southeast, you'll get a good view of the huge cottonwoods and willows clumped together in the protected Mormon Island Wetlands. Bring a good set of binoculars and a bird-watching book to spy a spectacular array of birds, from songbirds that stay in the area all year to migrating waterfowl.

You'll continue along the rocky shoreline contours, past gray pine and blue oaks, coming at 1.5 miles to a slender footpath that leads to a quaint cove. In spring, the lupine, vetch, and clover will all be in bloom.

So will the poison oak. You'll notice that this itchy plant grows as a ground cover, creeping vine, and shrub here. If your dog comes in contact with it, be sure to wash your pet off before getting back to your car, since a dog's fur can carry the itchy oils from the plant—and infect you days later (I know this from personal experience).

31. Loch Leven Lakes

Round trip: 5.4 miles
Hiking time: 3 hours or overnight
High point: 6850 feet
Elevation gain: 1120 feet
Best hiking time: Year-round; most in use mid-June to late October
Water: From Loch Leven Lakes
Maps: USGS Cisco Grove, USGS Soda Springs
Contact: Tahoe National Forest, Nevada City Ranger District,
     (530) 265-4531

Getting there: The trailhead and parking area are a short distance east of the Big Bend Ranger Station on Hampshire Rocks Road, which is off Interstate 80, about 75 miles northeast of Sacramento. Traveling east on I-80, take the Big Bend exit and turn left onto Hampshire Rocks Road. The signed trail begins on the south side of the road.

Winter, spring, summer, or fall, a trek to Loch Leven Lakes offers it all: Scenic overlooks. Muscle-burning uphills. Cool mountain lake swimming. Fishing. Or just plain sitting around. But you first have to get to this string of granite-basin lakes.

The first mile of this hike is steep, and will leave you and the dogs panting. It's a blessing, perhaps, that this section of trail is shaded by a lodgepole pine forest. You'll cross some Union Pacific Railroad tracks at 1.3 miles, where you'll see western white pine and the occasional quaking aspen.

Once you leave the forest, at 2.2 miles, the grade evens out; then you'll reach a series of switchbacks (make sure your dogs don't cut the switchbacks—this leads to erosion) that takes you to the top of a high ridge, where Lower Loch Leven Lake sits after 2.7 miles of hiking.

At the south end of the lake, the trail splits, with the branch to the

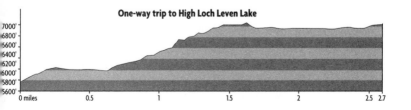

One-way trip to High Loch Leven Lake

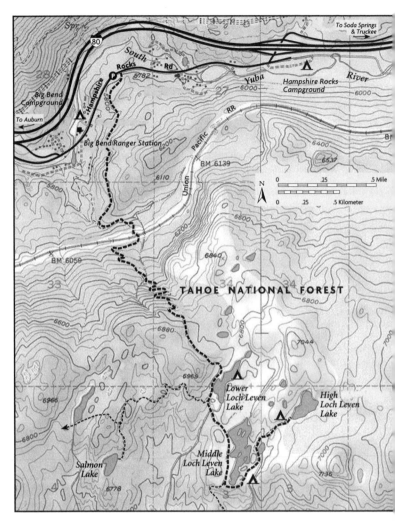

right leading southwest to Salmon Lake. The other fork continues south, climbing and descending small ridges to Middle Loch Leven. Keep going and you'll hit High Loch Leven Lake.

Camping is available at all the lakes, but you'll want to spend most of your time at High Loch Leven, which doesn't get as much pressure—and the granite-island-dotted shoreline is protected by white fir, red fir, lodgepole pine, and western white pine and provides much-appreciated shade in the summer. Fishing for brook and rainbow trout is good at all the lakes.

Be sure not to abandon this hike in the winter. While strenuous, the

trek on snowshoes offers a completely different perspective on the wilderness. Some cross-country skiers traverse the snow from the east on a marked trail to High Loch Leven, but most snowshoers reject the challenge. Don't

Anglers will love the trout fishing at Loch Level Lakes.

be one of them. Though with no trail to follow you'll need basic route-finding skills, finding the lakes isn't that big of a problem.

One thing to be aware of in winter is crossing the Union Pacific tracks. The company uses plow trains, which in heavy snow years can pile up a mound of snow that can't easily be climbed in snowshoes. It's generally a good idea to carry a snow shovel in the backcountry, and you can use it to dig steps in the snowbanks.

32. Caples Lake to Emigrant Lake

Round trip: 9 miles
Hiking time: 5 hours or overnight
High point: 8600 feet
Elevation gain: 950 feet
Best hiking time: Mid-July through late October
Water: From lakes
Map: USGS Caples Lake
Contact: Eldorado National Forest, Amador Ranger District, (209) 295-4251

Getting there: From the community of Meyers, at the junction of US 50 and Highway 89, drive south on Highway 89 for 11 miles to Highway

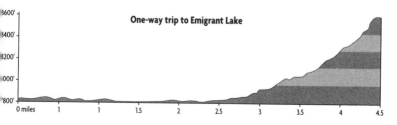

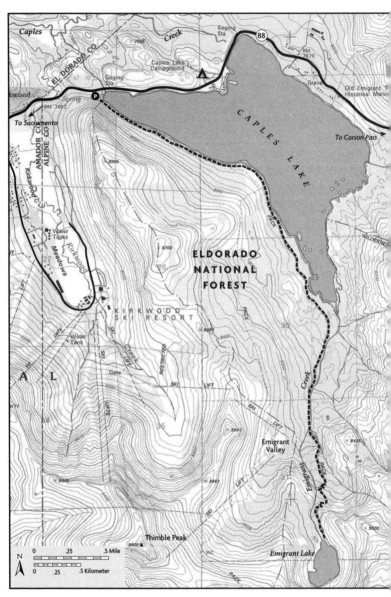

88. Turn west on Highway 88 and drive 14 miles to the west side of Caples Lake and the trailhead parking area, which is 5 miles west of the Carson Summit. The trailhead begins near the bathrooms. You'll need a wilderness permit to camp at Emigrant Lake, available from the Amador Ranger District.

Caples Lake (photo by Marc Soares)

This is a popular hike, since you'll get two great lakes—the first right outside your car door and the second after a surprisingly easy trek into the rugged, 105,165-acre Mokelumne Wilderness Area. This wilderness area, designated by Congress in 1964, straddles the crest of the central Sierra Nevada within the Stanislaus, Eldorado, and Toiyabe National Forests.

Because of increased outdoor activity near Carson Summit, officials with the Eldorado National Forest have had to place restrictions on an area known as the Carson Summit Management Area, which encompasses your destination, Emigrant Lake. As of this writing, people cannot camp within 300 feet of the lake so that the shoreline can heal. Also, campfires are not permitted. However, dogs are still allowed, and this is too scenic a trip to let rules that are good for the forest wreck your plans. Consider making this a day hike, instead of an overnighter.

Come in late summer and you'll have the opportunity to sample several great swimming spots. It is also possible to do this hike past the late-October date suggested; indeed, many people are finding that snowshoeing here—as well as snow camping—is a great way to visit the area minus the crowds. The Carson Summit Management Area plan states that you cannot camp unless there's at least a foot of snow on the ground, which usually is the case by Christmas. If you do opt for a snowshoe or cross-country adventure, make sure you have good map and compass skills, as well as having the foresight to pack winter survival gear that will get you to your destination and back.

The trail starts off among aspen and a mixed conifer forest of red fi. and lodgepole pine. At 1.2 miles, you'll see a sign for Emigrant Road, the trail that brought thousands of emigrants to California. From here, the trail crosses four seasonal creeks over the next 1.2 miles, each bordered by lush streamside plants like willow and alder. The path then links with Emigrant Creek as you finally bid farewell to Caples Lake.

You'll start to climb, gently, through a meadow where granite boul ders abound. Here, mountain hemlock comes into view, as the trail hug the creek thick with willows, and you'll come to a trail fork at 3.4 miles

At 4 miles, you'll get the chance to boulder-hop across Emigrant Lake's outlet stream, where you'll catch the first look at the Sisters' rocky spires At 4.3 miles, the trail levels out and parallels a small meadow. At 4.5 mile from the trailhead, you'll reach Emigrant Lake, set in a deep granite ba sin. Notice how the power of the glacier can literally move mountains From the lake's south shore, a talus-tumbled cliff rises nearly vertical from the water's edge.

33. Lake Margaret

Round trip: 5 miles
Hiking time: 3 hours or overnight
High point: 7750 feet
Elevation gain: 550 feet
Best hiking time: Early July through late October
Water: From streams and Lake Margaret
Map: USGS Caples Lake
Contact: Eldorado National Forest, Amador Ranger District,
  (209) 295-4251

Getting there: From the community of Meyers and the intersection o US 50 and Highway 89, drive south on Highway 89 for 11 miles to High way 88. Turn west on Highway 88 and drive 14.5 miles to the brown Forest Service sign that reads "Lake Margaret Trailhead" on the north side

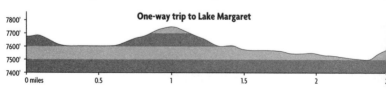

One-way trip to Lake Margaret

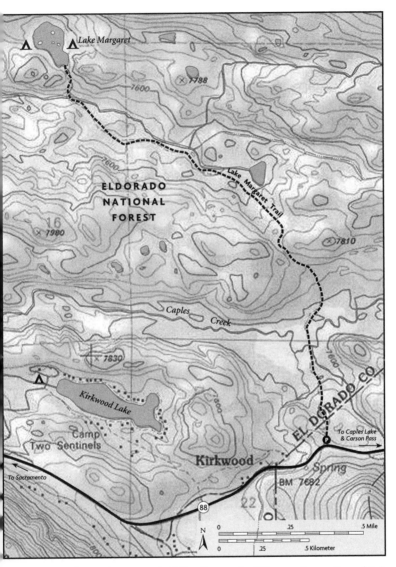

of the road. The parking area is 5.5 miles west of Carson Summit and 5.5 miles east of Silver Lake. You'll need to get a wilderness permit from the Eldorado National Forest (available at Amador Ranger District) if you plan on spending the night.

For little effort, this hike offers a lot of nature: a cool, inviting granite-basined alpine lake, a great burbling stream, and killer views. This is a trail built for children, families, and those households with a new puppy. Here, you'll get the chance to teach some leash lessons and get your new arrival used to hiking the trails of California and beyond.

The trail starts with a downhill trek through lodgepole pine and dense white fir toward a seasonal creek at just 0.2 mile. Here, the trail bends east; make sure to look straight ahead at the high mountain ridge just north of Caples Lake. The path parallels, then crosses, another seasonal stream and at a 0.5 mile you'll reach Caples Creek, where a grassy meadow makes for a perfect stop for a snack (and a quick dip in the clear creek waters).

You'll next climb a short grade (maybe 150 feet) bordered by granite hillsides. The trail levels out again and skirts a stagnant, lodgepole-and willow-choked pond on the left at 1.2 miles and immediately crosses more granite. A larger pond awaits at 1.6 miles. You'll soon cross a stream and pass through a dense mountain alder thicket. At 2.2 miles, aspen become your guardians along the path for nearly 300 yards, where you'll come to a stream that must be traversed across a log.

After getting past the log bridge, you'll hit your last ascent to the final destination. Here's where you'll follow cairns, or ducks—a pile of rocks that have been left by hikers to mark the trail—up the gently sloping granite hillside. After this short climb, you'll reach the cool, deep waters of Lake Margaret. This is a swimmer's paradise, as huge slabs of granite lie just below the water's surface, making it a great place to sit and soak up the abundant sunshine.

Campers will find two nice campsites on the lake's eastern shore, as well as two along the western shore. If you're lucky, you might even catch a few trout for cooking over a small warming fire.

Lake Margaret is a swimmer's (or dogpaddler's) paradise.

34. Crooked Lakes Trail to Penner Lake

Round trip: 6 miles
Hiking time: 3 hours or overnight
High point: 6900 feet
Elevation gain: 500 feet
Best hiking time: Mid-June through October
Water: From trailside lakes
Maps: USGS Graniteville, USGS English Mountain
Contact: Tahoe National Forest, Nevada City Ranger District, (530) 265-4531

Getting there: From the junction of Interstate 80 and Highway 20, take Highway 20 west for 4 miles, then turn north (right) onto Bowman Lake Road (Forest Road 18). Drive 8.4 miles on this paved road, then turn right at the sign for Carr Lake, where the trailhead is located. Stay on the main road and stay to the right at all road junctions along the last 2.7 miles. It gets a little bumpy along those last few miles, it's a dirt road, and the trailhead is located in the Carr Lake Campground.

Weekend solitude you'll not likely to find on this trail; however, if you want some of the most spectacular views of the Sierra Nevada and a string of alpine lakes where you can swim, fish, and sit and contemplate your navel (or any other worthy thoughts), this is the trail for you. You'll miss the crowds if you can trek midweek, but don't let a few people deter you from taking this hike. It's a drainer on the legs, no doubt, but the rewards are worth the effort.

The trail starts at the Carr Lake Campground, where you'll walk along the campground road going east until you cross a creek and turn onto the actual trail. That path hugs the shoreline of Feely Lake—favorite destination for anglers—where you'll get good views of Fall Creek Mountain to the north. After a 0.5 mile, you'll start to climb gradually, eventually leveling off at a small pond.

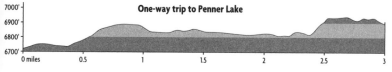

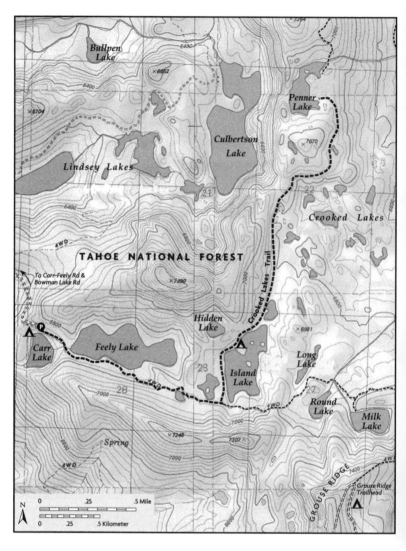

At 1 mile, you'll turn left onto the Crooked Lakes Trail, just after getting to an unnamed lake. The path goes between this lake to the left and Island Lake to the right.

Island Lake, along with Penner Lake, are the crown jewels of this hike. Both are spectacular in terms of beauty and play opportunities. Island Lake is encased in black-flecked granite, its crystal-clear waters inviting a quick dip. It's as if someone took a dipper into the blue Sierra Nevada sky and ladled it into a rock bowl. All around, the green of the red fir

Penner Lake offers great views of the Sierra Nevada.

and lodgepole pine forest sparkles and sets off the starkness of the serrated Sierra Nevada range.

If you can't pull yourself away, there are good campsites amid the lodgepole pines near the water's edge to the left. These are fairly popular sites, so if they're full, try one of several sites along the east shore.

After bidding Island Lake farewell at 1.5 miles, you'll enter a cool red fir forest, where you'll come upon a small waterfall coming from Island Lake's outlet. The first of the Crooked Lakes comes at 2 miles, but it's shallow, marshy, and there are better choices ahead. The path starts to lose elevation at 2.3 miles, where you'll pick up a side trail on the right of the lake that leads to another small lake. Follow this path along the creek to the best of the Crooked Lakes, a large, deep, granite-encased pool. There's one good campsite where the side trail ends.

If Penner Lake is your destination, stay on the Crooked Lakes Trail, where you'll climb steadily for 0.5 mile of rocky terrain. At 2.8 miles, you'll crest the ridge and see the expansive, rocky shores of Penner below. Hopefully, you can stay for the alpenglow sunset on this lake.

It's also the best fishing lake in this string; the California Department of Fish and Game plants fingerling rainbow trout here every year, which can almost assure a trout dinner for the dedicated angler. Campsites are hard to come by at Penner, but if you don't mind pitching your tent on a slab of granite, the views can't be beat.

SAN FRANCISCO BAY AREA

35. South Beach Trail

Round trip: 0.5–20 miles
Hiking time: 20 minutes–8 hours
High point: Sea level
Elevation gain: Negligible
Best hiking time: Year-round; low fog is common in summer
Water: From drinking fountain at the trailhead
Map: USGS Drakes Bay
Contact: Point Reyes National Seashore, (415) 464-5100

Getting there: From US 101 in Marin, take the Sir Francis Drake Boulevard exit and drive about 20 miles west to the town of Olema. Turn right on Highway 1 and drive a short distance to Bear Valley Road. Turn left on Bear Valley Road and drive 2 miles. Turn left on Sir Francis Drake Boulevard and drive 11.6 miles to the access turnoff for the South Beach parking lot to the right. Park for free near the bathrooms; several trails lead down to the beach.

Point Reyes National Seashore is a national treasure—where dogs are pretty much not allowed. Except for South Beach, an untouched beachfront where people can bring their pets, so as long as there are no marine mammals on the beach. If seals are present, the pooch has to stay in the car.

This is one of those make-your-own-adventure hikes. Stay close to the parking area on the beach, pull out a blanket for a picnic, and take it

One-way trip on Point Reyes Beach

50'
0'
0 miles   1   2   3

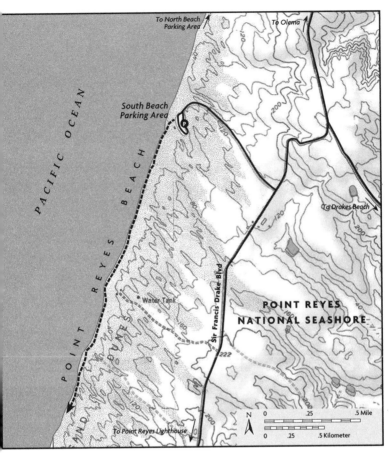

easy. Roam the sandy hillsides that are covered with ice plants (blooms of yellow, orange, pink, purple, and red will amaze you).

Or, for the best hike, reach the beach and turn south for about a mile until you come to the sand dunes, stopping every so often to find out what the ocean has brought to shore. When we were there, we found bits of sand-blasted glass (an artist friend made me swear I'd look), shells, boat floats in several colors, and one big, dead cabazon, a deep ocean fish. You can even go as far as you'd like on the beach. Some days, it may be just you and your dog on this stretch, where the Pacific meets California.

A note about the water: don't go swimming, and watch for rogue waves. The area is known for its tremendous undertow, which will take even the strongest dog paddler under and out to sea, despite all attempts to swim back in.

Ice plants in a variety of colors cover the sandy hills at Point Reyes National Seashore.

Oh, and on your way in on Sir Francis Drake Boulevard, don't miss the chance to pick up some fresh oysters and talk about oyster farming at Johnson's Oyster Company. You'll see the sign and turnoff; the store is open from 8:00 a.m. to 4:30 p.m. and is closed Mondays.

36. Bolinas Ridge

Round trip: Up to 11 miles
Hiking time: 4–6 hours
High point: 1300 feet
Elevation gain: 1100 feet
Best hiking time: Year-round
Water: Bring your own
Maps: USGS Iverness, USGS San Geronimo
Contact: Golden Gate National Recreation Area, (415) 556-0561 or (415) 663-1092

Getting there: From US 101 in San Rafael, take the Sir Francis Drake Boulevard exit and go west for 17 miles (3.4 miles past Samuel P. Taylor

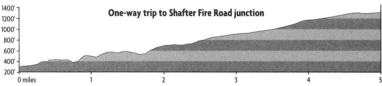

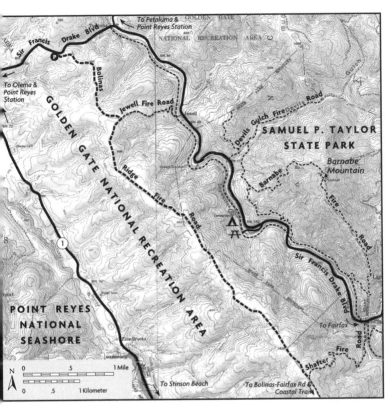

State Park's entrance). The trailhead is on the left side of the road, where the parking is free. Alternately, from the community of Olema on Highway 1, drive 1.1 miles east on Sir Francis Drake Boulevard.

If sweeping views and a certain amount of solitude are your idea of a weekend escape, the Bolinas Ridge Trail just might be your cup of tea. The trail is open to hikers, mountain bikers, and leashed dogs, of course.

The trail starts from a wooden gate and gains 700 feet in elevation is the first 2.5 miles, cutting through rough granite outcroppings as the wide and inviting path inches up the ridgeline. You'll come to your first spot to look around at a little over 0.5 mile. Look northwest for good views of Tomales Bay and the Point Reyes peninsula. Look east to Barnabe Peak (Hike 37).

At 1.3 miles, you'll get to a signed trail junction for the Jewell Fire Road. A little farther on, you'll come to a field that from which you can see the dark forested Iverness Ridge as well as the Olema Valley. The trail gains its highest point nearly 5 miles into the trek, where eucalyptus trees stand guard.

Grazing is allowed on Bolinas Ridge, so dog walkers need to be aware of the local bovine residents.

But the best place to look around is at the junction with the Shafter Fire Road, where you can scramble up any knoll for great views of Iverness Ridge and the Pacific. From here, it's 0.5 mile to the left to reach Lagunitas Creek, where the dogs can cool off and you can get out of the sun and rest in a canopy of dense oak and bay laurel. After a rest, maybe a little lunch, just retrace your steps back to the trailhead.

A note of caution: the recreation area allows cattle grazing, so make sure to keep control of your dog, as cows can get downright nasty if harassed.

37. Barnabe Peak

Round trip: 3 miles
Hiking time: 3–5 hours
High point: 1466 feet
Elevation gain: 1300 feet
Best hiking time: Year-round
Water: From Devils Gulch and Lagunitas Creeks; or bring your own
Map: USGS San Geronimo
Contact: Samuel P. Taylor State Park, (415) 488-9897

Getting there: From US 101 in San Rafael, drive 13 miles west on Sir Francis Drake Boulevard. Park for free on the south side of the road, 0.9 mile past the entrance to Samuel P. Taylor State Park. Alternately, from Olema on Highway 1, take Sir Francis Drake Boulevard east 6 miles.

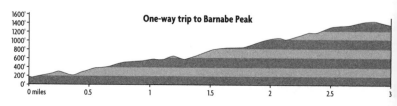

Most people who take on this hike include a side trip to Stairstep Falls, which in winter through spring tumbles down 10 feet of dark rock. Alas, dogs are only allowed on the park's fire roads, which knocks out a side trip to the falls.

Start this hike by crossing Sir Francis Drake Boulevard and walking a couple of hundred yards up an asphalt path along Devils Gulch Creek. Go to campsite 2, turn right, and pick up the slender dirt path signed for Barnabe Peak (you'll notice the sign, since it is clearly marked that dogs must be leashed). You'll cross a wooden bridge to the forested side of the creek (the dogs can splash right through the creek).

The trail climbs out of the canyon and breaks from a canopy of bay laurel, redwoods, live oak, red alder, and the occasional coffeeberry and hazelnut. Then it hits you: in the next 2.5 miles, you'll gain 1100 feet of elevation, while the trail (now a fire road) seems to make an endless zigzag of switchbacks. In the spring, the hills are lush and green, with plenty of California poppy and lupine to gander at.

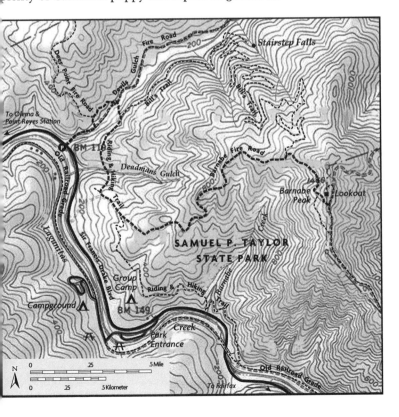

The view from just below Barnabe Peak

Your destination is the rugged stone lookout on Barnabe Peak. As the trail ascends, you'll get a good look at Bolinas Ridge (Hike 36) and San Geronimo Ridge (Hike 39). Once you make the top, stop to rest and take in the sweeping, 360-degree views before heading back to your car.

Just before settling back into the shade of the bay laurel, take a left at a signed trail junction to check out the gravesite of mill owner and miner Samuel P. Taylor. Back on the trail, you'll hook up with the Devils Gulch Fire Road and make your way out to the asphalt trail.

38. Roys Redwoods Trail

Round trip: 3-mile loop
Hiking time: 2–3 hours
High point: 800 feet
Elevation gain: 500 feet
Best hiking time: Year-round
Water: Bring your own
Map: USGS San Geronimo
Contact: Marin County Open Space District, (415) 499-6387

Getting there: From a few miles west of Fairfax on Sir Francis Drake Boulevard, turn north onto Nicasio Valley Road. Drive 0.4 mile and park for free on the side of the road, by the outhouses.

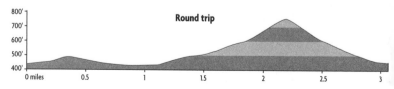

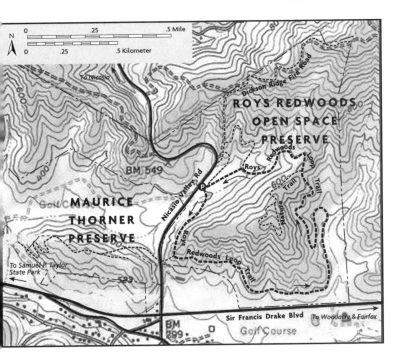

Here's a happy little trail that passes through a pleasant meadow, dives into a darkened forest of giant redwoods, and comes back out again. There's no destination here, just a carefree little jaunt where you're likely to strike

up any number of conversations with people who stop to walk this tiny strip of open space.

The trail starts just north of the outhouses. It skirts the meadow just below Nicasio Valley Road and heads beneath Roys Redwoods, towering giants with lightning-scarred trunks. Entering this forest, you'll see bay laurel and madrone; ferns and poison oak rule the underbrush.

Soon enough, the trail breaks

Coastal Redwoods tower over a meadow in Roys Redwoods Open Space Preserve.

from the forest and heads into a mix of grassland and sagebrush that alternates with stands of coast live oak. Take the trail that climbs (stay to the left) at each of the next two junctions. That way, you'll alternate between rocky outcrops and pretty little meadows that are ablaze with wildflowers in the spring.

Stay on course to a nearly bald top and a grassy ridge for a look around. The trail now veers east, stays high for a bit, then drops back toward the meadow. The trail loops back into the redwoods, were you'll be hard pressed not to play a little hide-and-seek with the dogs as they sniff around the many delectable scents.

39. San Geronimo Ridge

Round trip: 3–7 miles
Hiking time: 3–5 hours
High point: 1400 feet
Elevation gain: 700 feet
Best hiking time: Year-round
Water: Bring your own
Map: USGS Bolinas
Contact: Marin County Open Space District, (415) 499-6387

Getting there: From US 101 in San Rafael, take Sir Francis Drake Boulevard to Fairfax. Continue west through Fairfax for 4 miles and take Railroad Avenue (it's signed for Woodacre) south. Go 0.7 mile and turn right on Carson Road. Follow this narrow, paved road through a residential neighborhood and ignore the first Conifer Way fork. After a mile, take a very sharp left onto Conifer Way, climb another 0.2 mile and park for free near the brown pipe gate that signals the trailhead, as well as a dead-end to the road.

Residential neighborhoods seem to be closing in everywhere, as the squeeze to fit more people into California (the population is expected

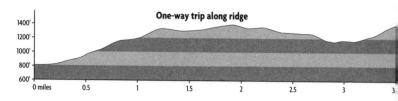

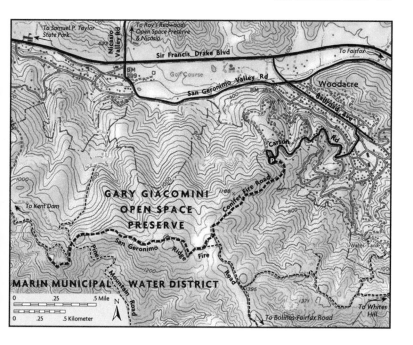

to top 54 million by 2050) collides with the needs of people to recreate in clean, green open spaces. Marin County is dotted with open spaces, parcels of land where forward-thinking people decided no development would take place. These would instead be left as places where people could ride mountain bikes, stroll with their dogs, or even get out on horseback.

The Gary Giacomini Open Space Preserve is one such area—of many— that surrounds the hip town of Fairfax. Here, you'll gain about 700 feet in elevation for a nice little workout and spectacular views from atop San Geronimo Ridge.

Start on Conifer Fire Road, go past a water tower and through a forest of Douglas fir, bay laurel, and live oak. After breaking from the woods, turn southwest for a view of the small community of Woodacre. At the top of the ridge crest, a spur trail wanders north and leads to a striking view of the San Geronimo Valley. I took this trek as the sun was setting, and the ridge made for a rare show as the sun sank toward the Pacific.

To the west, you'll link up with San Geronimo Ridge Fire Road, an old dirt road that travels through a mix of coyote brush and rare Tamalpais manzanita. Meander along this trail for as long or as little as you like. When you've had your fill of a little open space, retrace your steps to

The view from San Geronimo Ridge.

your car—and maybe a stop for a cold beverage in Fairfax's funky, inviting downtown, where dogs are as common as window shoppers.

40. Cascade Falls Trail

Round trip: 1.8 miles
Hiking time: 1 hour
High point: 400 feet
Elevation gain: negligible
Best hiking time: Year-round
Water: From San Anselmo Creek; or bring your own
Map: USGS Bolinas
Contact: Marin County Open Space District, (415) 499-6387

Getting there: From US 101 in San Rafael, take Sir Francis Drake Boulevard west to the town of Fairfax. Turn left onto Claus Drive, then make an immediate left onto Broadway, followed by an immediate right onto Bolinas Road. Drive 0.3 mile to a three-way intersection, where you'll take the middle road (Cascade Drive) for 1.5 miles. Park near the gate to the Elliott Nature Preserve, but watch for the no-parking signs in this residential area and be sure not to block any driveways.

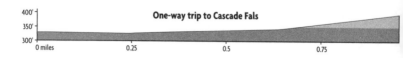

It's not the most powerful waterfall you'll likely see in your life, more like a gurgling friend, a quiet spot to rest, relax, and step out of the rat race, if only for the hour it takes to wander though Cascade Canyon Open Space Preserve and the Elliott Nature Preserve. But make no mistake about it, happy Cascade Falls is worth the trip; indeed during my first trek there, numerous harried people asked if they were getting close the falls, which tumble down San Anselmo Creek before it wid-

Lilies line the shaded trail to Cascade Falls.

ens out and provides a couple of great dipping spots for the dogs.

The trail starts at a sign for the Elliott Nature Preserve. You'll want to ignore all unsigned trail junctions and stick to the creek, which you'll cross at 0.5 mile on a wooden bridge. Continue going straight (you'll be

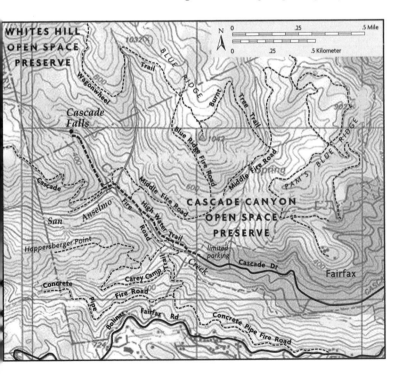

on the creek's left side) and go deeper into Cascade Canyon, where currant and madrone make up the cozy canopy.

Through the canyon, San Anselmo Creek will narrow, and the gurgling will start to echo off the cliff walls. You'll end up at Cascade Falls in about a mile. The falls are encased in a rocky, moss-covered grotto, where large boulders make for a great spot to stop and contemplate your navel (hey, it's so peaceful that you really don't need to be thinking of anything).

After a few quiet moments, retrace your steps to your car, but be sure to reward your dog for waiting while you got a little Zen with a quick dip in San Anselmo Creek.

41. Alpine Lake Trail

Round trip: 5.2-mile loop
Hiking time: 3 hours
High point: 1200 feet
Elevation gain: 800 feet
Best hiking time: Year-round
Water: At the trailhead; or from Alpine Lake
Maps: USGS San Rafael, Marin Municipal Water District map
Contact: Marin Municipal Water District, Sky Oaks Ranger Station,
(415) 945-1181

Getting there: From the Golden Gate Bridge, take US 101 north and turn west onto Sir Francis Drake Boulevard to Fairfax. Turn left on Claus Drive, make an immediate left onto Broadway, and then turn right onto Bolinas Road. Travel on Bolinas Road for 1.4 miles, turn left on Sky Oaks Road (where you'll stop at the Sky Oaks Ranger Station to pay the $5 day-use fee and pick up a free water district map), and follow Sky Oaks 2 miles to the parking area at the base of Bon Tempe Dam. Pick up the Kewt Trail to the south along Rocky Ridge Fire Road.

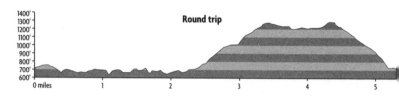

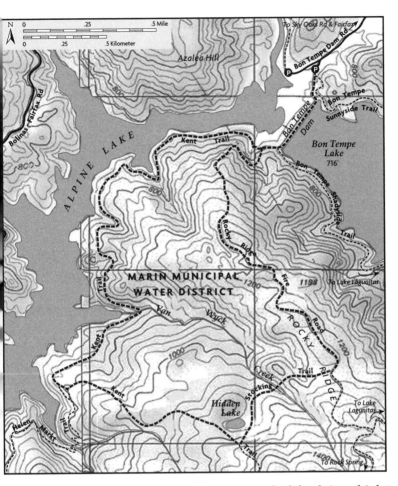

This area is managed as part of a 24,000-acre watershed that brings drinking water to 246,073 people in Marin County, but you could have fooled me—the sprawling area includes five lakes stocked with trout, forested hills, and 130 acres of maintained trails.

The area was purchased in 1918 from the Marin Water and Power Company and has evolved into the water-storage and recreation site it is today. Rain that falls on Mount Tamalpais flows into Lagunitas Creek and its tributaries and is stored in the water district's five reservoirs. Lake Lagunitas (Hike 42) was built in 1872, Phoenix Lake (Hike 46) in 1905, Alpine Lake in 1918 (enlarged in 1924 and 1941), Bon Tempe Lake in 1948, and Kent Lake in 1953. Each has its own distinctive vibe, but Alpine really stands out.

The trail hugs the shoreline of Alpine Lake before turning into the forest.

The largest of the lakes, Alpine looks like it was sliced out of the Sierra Nevada and plopped down in these hills just north of San Francisco. The trout tend to be bigger in Alpine than in the other lakes—catch-and-release fishing is encouraged—and can average about 15 inches (so anglers, make sure you bring those pack rods, this hike leads to some pretty secluded inlets).

This hike takes dogs and their owners along the shoreline of the lake, up through the redwoods to Hidden Lake and Rocky Point (where the views are spectacular), and then back down to Bon Tempe Lake and Dam.

The trail meanders through the pines and redwoods along the lake, and finally turns inland, where the redwoods block much of the sunlight and the world turns green with maidenhair and sword ferns.

At Hidden Lake, a cattail-choked pond, the scene changes as you pick up the sun-drenched Stocking Trail. From the dense forest, the scene changes to rocky outcrops, skittering fence lizards, manzanita thickets, and live oaks. You'll pick up the Rocky Ridge Fire Road Trail (Stocking Trail dead ends) and follow this wide path back to Bon Tempe Dam.

42. Two Lakes Trail

Round trip: 5 miles
Hiking time: 2.5 hours
High point: 740 feet
Elevation gain: 80 feet
Best hiking time: Year-round; streams might not be passable in early spring
Water: From Lagunitas and Bon Tempe Lakes
Map: USGS Bolinas, Marin Municipal Water District map
Contact: Marin Municipal Water District, Sky Oaks Ranger Station, (415) 945-1181

Getting there: From the Golden Gate Bridge, take US 101 north and turn west onto Sir Francis Drake Boulevard to Fairfax. Turn left on Claus Drive, make an immediate left onto Broadway, and turn right onto Bolinas Road. Travel on Bolinas Road for 1.4 miles, turn left on Sky Oaks Road (where you'll stop at the Sky Oaks Ranger Station to pay the $5 day-use fee and pick up a free water district map), and follow Sky Oaks 0.25 mile to a signed fork to the Lagunitas parking area.

Every happy person I know has a favorite lake or pond from childhood; maybe it's the water, but people who have grown up skipping stones, hunting salamanders, casting a line, or sticking their toes in chilled waters tend to have sunnier dispositions. Take your entire family—dogs included—to this spot, and give them a strong foundation in life.

This hike actually is the best of two lakes; many of the locals call this trek the "Two Lakes Trail" since you'll start at Lagunitas and get the best views of Bon Tempe as you head back to your car. The trick is to do the Lagunitas Lake Fire Road counterclockwise, then link up with the Pilot Knob Trail, hike past the parking area, and then along the Bon Tempe Shadyside Trail.

The Lagunitas Lake Fire Road is intimate and shaded, providing a stroll that skirts the shoreline and jumps a few seasonal streams. You'll pick

Round trip to Lagunitas and Bon Tempe Lakes

Cattails frame Lake Lagunitas, where trout fishing is allowed.

up the Bon Tempe Shadyside Trail at 1.1 miles. This slim dirt path give
the best views of the area as it traverses through the coast live oak forest
and three canyons.

You'll reach a three-way junction at 2.2 miles, where a short jaunt

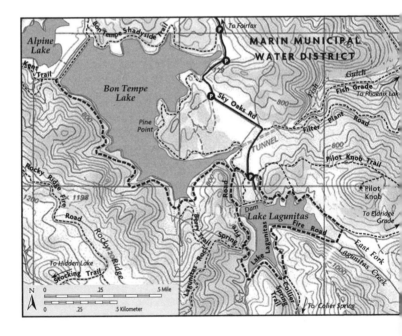

down a dirt road leads to a great photo opportunity of Bon Tempe Lake and Mount Tamalpais; this spot is the only place where you can see both Bon Tempe and Alpine Lakes together.

43. Cataract Falls and Laurel Dell

Round trip: 2.5 miles
Hiking time: 1.5 hours
High point: 1670 feet
Elevation gain: 1030 feet
Best hiking time: Winter through spring; hikable year-round
Water: From Cataract Creek, or bring your own
Map: USGS French Gulch
Contact: Marin Municipal Water District, Sky Oaks Ranger Station, (415) 945-1181

Getting there: From the Golden Gate Bridge, take US 101 north and turn west onto Sir Francis Drake Boulevard to Fairfax. Turn left on Claus Drive, make an immediate left onto Broadway, and turn right onto Bolinas-Fairfax Road. Drive 8.2 twisty miles to Alpine Dam, cross it, and look for the parking area just before a tight, right-hand hairpin turn. Park for free off the road; the trailhead starts on the other side of the road.

It's a gut-wrenching climb that makes sweat pour down your forehead, and even the stoutest dog will have its tongue extended fully, but Cataract Falls and the Laurel Dell Picnic Area are worth every pounding heartbeat. For Cataract Falls isn't just one falls, but a set of cascading waterfalls that rush down a wooded ravine on the slopes of Mount Tamalpais.

The sights and smells are worth the sweat equity you'll expend on this 750-foot-elevation climb. Besides, the picnic area is a welcomed pit stop where you can spread out a blanket and have a feast (go ahead and pack carbs, you'll burn them).

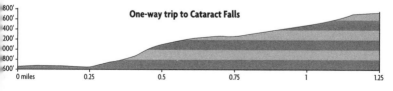

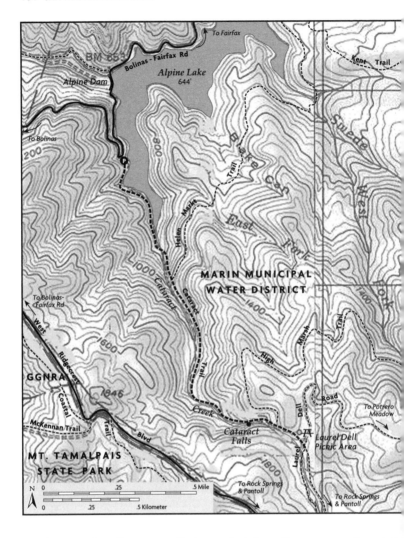

The signed trail starts to climb gently (where there are good spots to cast a line along the shores of Alpine Lake). The well-covered trail offers a canopy of redwood, bigleaf maple, tan oak, and hazelnut. Don't be deceived. At a little more than 0.5 mile, where huckleberries and ferns are thick, you'll come to a trail junction (stay straight) where the climbing commences. The roar of the falls takes over as the water tumbles down the canyon. It's a restful beat to climb to, as you constantly come to new and higher steps cut into the canyon.

At 1.4 miles, a spur trail takes you to the best view of the falls, where water slips, slides, and cascades down slick boulders into inviting pools. During the wet months, Cataract Creek becomes a whitewater torrent, with foam and spray and a roar that can drown out conversation with someone standing right next to you.

Cataract Creek is peaceful as it comes into Alpine Lake.

A little ways up, you'll hit Laurel Dell, a wide, open spot surrounded by coast live oak, bigleaf maple, bay laurel, and Douglas fir. Stay as long as you like (remember that it might be tough to find a spot on the weekends), then retrace your steps back down to Alpine Dam. Or continue on a longer, steeper hike up Mount Tam (Hike 44).

44. Mount Tamalpais East Peak Trail

Round trip: 13 miles
Hiking time: 6–8 hours
High point: 2571 feet
Elevation gain: 2300 feet
Best hiking time: Year-round
Water: Bring plenty of your own
Maps: USGS San Rafael, USGS Bolinas
Contact: Marin Municipal Water District, (415) 924-4600 or (415) 459-5267

Getting there: From Sir Francis Drake Boulevard in Fairfax, turn southeast on Claus Drive. Take an immediate left onto Broadway and then an

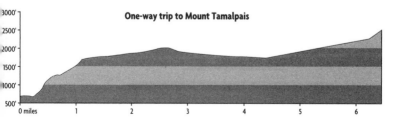

immediate right onto Bolinas-Fairfax Road. Drive 8.2 twisty miles, cross the Alpine Dam, and park for free at the hairpin turn. The signed trail begins on the left side of the road.

So the ranger says, "If you really want a nice hike up Mount Tam, try this route up Colier Springs Trail to the Northside Trail. Inspiration Point has some killer views and it's a good route to the top, not too strenuous."

It's a hike to the top of Mount Tamalpais.

Mount Tam, or Tamalpais, is the Bay Area's beloved "Sleeping Maiden." It towers 2,571 feet above the congestion and development that is the Bay Area. The area is a breath of fresh air, an open space for the masses. On one side, there's the Marin Municipal Water District's 18,500-acre open space area. On the other is the 6300-acre Mount Tamalpais State Park.

Mount Tam is actually three peaks on one ridge, with East Peak being the tallest. I decided that the most direct route—the very one suggested by the nice ranger who gave my dog Trinity a dog biscuit—didn't fit my particular needs (to be honest, I couldn't find the trailhead among the myriad of trails in the open space). No, I started from the one trailhead I knew, from the base of Alpine Dam, past lovely Cataract Falls and a great pit stop at Laurel Dell Picnic Area.

This East Peak route is a heart-pounding assault through a dense forest of redwood, tan oak, bigleaf maple, and hazelnut. It's the one trail with about 2300 feet of climbing (I am not kidding. The dam sits at 644 feet) The trail gains 750 feet just to Cataract Falls, in just under 1.5 miles. It's also a trail that's dog-friendly (just be sure to keep your dog on a leash—it's the rule, not a suggestion). Be prepared to sweat. Pack plenty of water, a hearty lunch, and some dog treats. And don't forget a camera.

This trek has it all: pristine forest, a lake full of fish, a cascading falls (winter and spring), a great picnic area at an historic outdoor theater and inn, and jaw-dropping views of San Pablo and San Francisco Bays. (Be sure to stay on the trails and fire roads; it's kinda like cheating if you hoof it up paved Ridgecrest Boulevard to the top.)

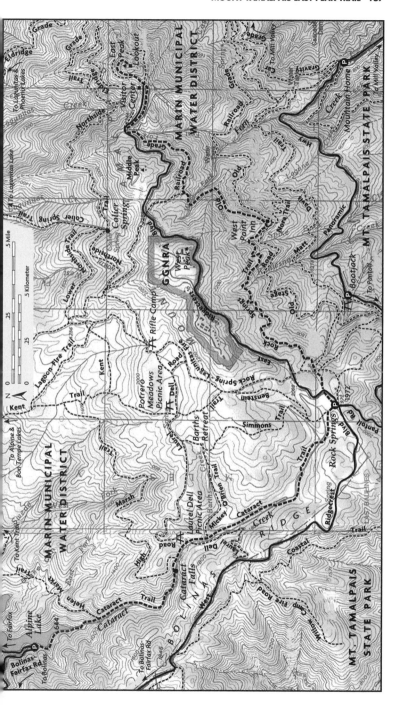

At least you'll have the option to rest at the pretty Laurel Dell Picnic Area, a large clearing with plenty of room to spread out. The area is framed by coast live oak, bay laurel, Douglas fir, and bigleaf maple.

From the picnic area, continue on the Cataract Trail 1.3 miles to Rock Springs Picnic Area. Be sure not to miss the Mountain Theater, a 3500-seat open amphitheater made of stone. To get there, cross Ridgecrest Boulevard and follow the signs to the theater, then rejoin the Rock Springs Trail. The trip up to East Peak also features a jaunt past West Point Inn at 4.5 miles. This is a neat stone lodge tucked in the forest, where you'll get great views of Angel Island and the Golden Gate Bridge.

Resume your trek to the top by finding the signed Old Railroad Grade Fire Road Trail and be sure to stop for a striking photo opportunity: Douglas fir in the foreground and Alcatraz Island, the Bay Bridge, and San Francisco's towering downtown in the background. The old dirt road stays fairly level through open chaparral until it reaches the Mount Tam visitor center. From the parking lot, hike the final 400 feet up a rocky trail to the terminus at East Peak.

There, take your pick of boulders, pop open a water bottle, and drink in the sweeping, 360-degree views.

45. Pine Mountain Summit

Round trip: 5.8 miles
Hiking time: 3–5 hours
High point: 1762 feet
Elevation gain: 1100 feet
Best hiking time: Winter through spring; hikable year-round
Water: Bring your own
Map: USGS Bolinas
Contact: Marin Municipal Water District, Sky Oaks Ranger Station, (415) 945-1181

Getting there: From Sir Francis Drake Boulevard in Fairfax, turn southeast on Claus Drive. Take an immediate left onto Broadway and an immediate

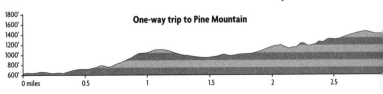

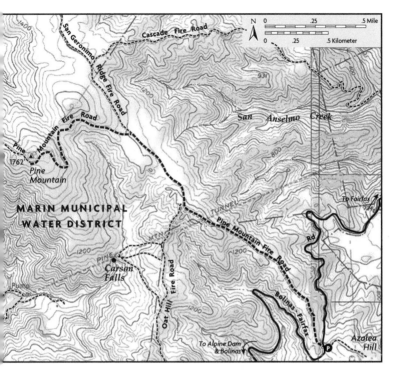

right onto Bolinas-Fairfax Road. Drive 3.8 twisty miles to a parking turnout on the left. The signed trail starts across the road (watch for cars).

Another trek with 1100 feet of elevation gain?

Hey, the whole idea is get out with your dog and get a little exercise. This trail, however, is more than just a sweaty excuse to get outdoors. Pine Mountain is a beautiful trek where a wide fire road winds its way up through low-growing chaparral—like chamise and ceanothus—coast live oaks, madrones, and twisted boulder outcroppings. If you hike this trail at certain times of the year (and certain times of the day), you might only see a couple of mountain bikers taking the challenge to get to the top; but the top is where you'll want to be, for sweeping views of Mount Diablo, San Pablo Bay, Alpine Lake, and Mount Tamalpais.

The first 0.5 mile starts out easy enough, slowly winding up from the parking lot and through a sea of boulders and bunchgrass. The climb then steepens, heads past some huge boulders, and hits a trail junction at 1 mile. Bear left onto signed Oat Hill Road. This dirt fire road gives you

The rugged trail, with Pine Mountain Summit as a destination.

your first good look at Pine Mountain to the west—and what the terrain will be like getting there.

A little past this point, about 0.2 mile farther on, there's an unsigned trail bearing right that heads down to Carson Falls (right beneath the power pole). Although nice to look at in the wet months, I don't recommend this side trip for dog owners, unless you've packed your dog's booties. The trail is slender and there's a lot of weather-beaten granite to contend with. That said, the falls is a series of five waterfalls that make up a cascade of water over the rough granite. It's 1.5 miles to the falls from Oat Hill Road.

Continuing up, you'll be amazed at the mix of chaparral and meadow the trail passes through. In spring, the hills become Technicolor with the blooming wildflowers, including lupine, wild iris, and California poppy. The trail actually levels out a bit as you reach a grassy plain, at about 2.8 miles. Here, you'll turn left and start the steep climb to dome-shaped Pine Mountain.

There are plenty of places to rest, out of the sea breezes that blow in. And be sure to get the camera ready, since you'll have views of the ocean and several ridges and lakes that make up the area.

46. Phoenix Lake

Round trip: 4.2 miles
Hiking time: 3 hours
High point: 350 feet
Elevation gain: 200 feet
Best hiking time: Year-round
Water: At the trailhead and one bathroom stop
Map: USGS San Rafael
Contact: Marin Municipal Water District, Sky Oaks Ranger Station,
(415) 945-1181

Getting there: From US 101 in San Rafael, take the Sir Francis Drake Boulevard exit, drive west to the community of Ross, and turn left on Lagunitas Road. Drive 1.3 miles and park for free in a large parking lot at the end of the drive. You'll pick up the trail just past the bridge (just follow the other dogs).

If you have a dog who "loves to read the signs," gentle Phoenix Lake is the place to be. This 4.2-mile trip is a dog walker's heaven, where friendly people ask—often—if their dogs can meet your dogs. After a few minutes of sniffing (by dogs, of course), you'll be on your way until the next encounter.

Phoenix Lake was created in 1905 when ranchers built the dam, which created the reservoir. History has it that the dam was going to be put up over the old Shaver stage coach line, cutting off the dairies from Ross Station so that the ranchers would have to make the more tedious run over the hills to Fairfax. There were some threats, some guns pulled, and in a compromise, a road was built across the dam and up the canyon. It's this road where the hike begins.

The Marin Municipal Water District now maintains the 25-acre lake, which has some good fishing for bass and trout (the Marin Rod and Gun Club, along with the water district, manages the lake as a self-sustaining

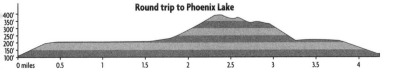

Round trip to Phoenix Lake

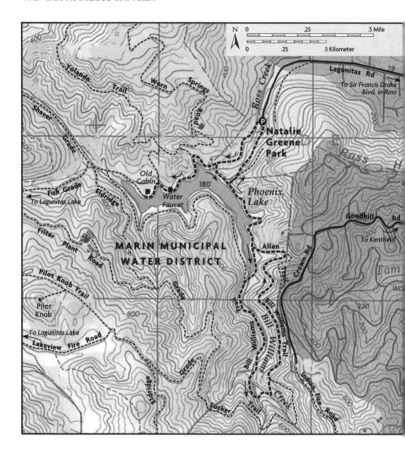

black bass fishery). In the fall, the leaves all turn orange and red and in the spring, wildflowers bloom all over. In between, manzanita—with its cool, mint-green leaves and mahogany-colored bark—and ferns make up the color palate.

The first part of the hike (going west) takes you past an old redwood cabin, which was built by James and Janet Porteous for their coachman and which predates the reservoir by twelve years. The cabin is unique and was the only building left standing after a fire destroyed the Porteous estate in the 1920s. The building has been vacant for more than sixty years, but it was restored in 1989.

Heading back to the east, past the trail to the parking area, the single-track Allen Trail takes hikers into a small canyon dotted with bay laurel, buckeye, and coast live oak. The area opens up to a grassy swath once you get to the Bill Williams Trail a bit farther on. Supposedly, Williams

Sunset and Trinity at Phoenix Lake

was a Confederate Army deserter who mined gold on the creek where his cabin stood. One of the big mysteries is that Williams hid all his treasure somewhere in the canyons, where it is said to remain today. Indeed, people tell stories that workers building the dam spent more time digging for the treasure than working on the project.

However, the real treasure here is the hike, which winds back to Natalie Greene Park down a single-track road and your vehicle.

47. Deer Island

Round trip: 3-mile loop
Hiking time: 1 hour
High point: 250 feet
Elevation gain: 200 feet
Best hiking time: September through June
Water: Bring your own
Map: USGS Petaluma Point
Contact: Marin County Open Space District, (415) 499-6387

Getting there: Drive US 101 north 2.6 miles past Highway 37 and take the Atherton/San Marin exit. Go east on Atherton and after 1.8 miles,

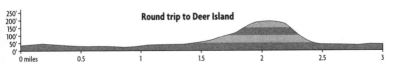

Oaks dot the Deer Island Open Space Preserve.

turn right on Olive Avenue, then left on Deer Island Lane. After 0.5 mile, you'll reach a gravel parking area, where you can park for free. The trail starts just past the trash can and wood gate.

If you're not a local, you'll swear we're leading you along here. In a mix of new, grand estates, thirty-year-old ranch homes, and a strip mall, no way will you think there was any place around to enjoy a little open space in this built-up area north of San Francisco.

But the Deer Island Open Space Preserve is a little sliver of heaven. Joggers use the trail, as do hikers, horseback riders, and dog walkers. It really is an island that rises slightly above the surrounding wetlands. In the spring, when the oaks are leafing out and the grass is green, you'll have the added thrill of looking down at the birdlife that will be searching for food in the flooded fields.

To start, go east on the packed-dirt trail and head directly into a hardwood forest of bay laurel and oak, where massive trees look as wide as they are tall. After 0.5 mile, turn right and begin a 200-foot climb to the signed De Borba Trail and the first of many sweeping vistas. As soon as you reach the Deer Island Ridge, you'll bear left onto the Arnold Baptiste

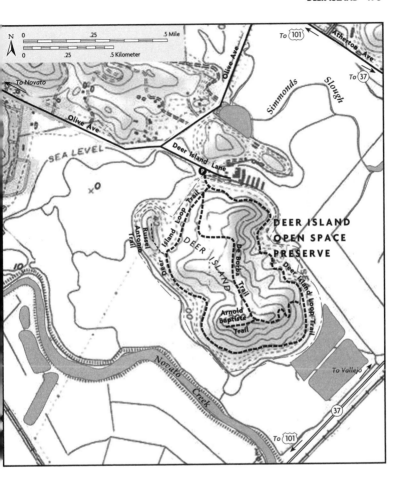

Trail, which leads to a grassy knoll. This is the best place to stretch out and have a snack.

Double-back and continue to ridge-hike on the De Borba Trail, where you'll find a massive, moss-covered boulder at a ridgetop junction. Here's where the sweeping views get really good, with swanky developments in Novato, Mount Diablo, and San Pablo Bay in the distance.

To complete the loop, backtrack a bit to the southern junction with the Deer Island Loop Trail at 1.8 miles. This 1.2-mile trek passes by some historic old corrals and offers the best views of the surrounding wetlands. If you have the time, take the longer loop around the island's perimeter. If time is short, continue north instead of heading back to the ridgetop. The trail will drop back to the trailhead in about a 0.25 mile.

48. Mount Burdell

Round trip: 6.2 miles
Hiking time: 3–5 hours
High point: 1550 feet
Elevation gain: 1400 feet
Best hiking time: Year-round
Water: Bring your own
Maps: USGS Petaluma River, USGS Novato
Contact: Marin County Open Space District, (415) 499-6387

Getting there: Drive US 101 north 2.6 miles past Highway 37, take the Atherton/San Marin exit, and go west on San Marin Drive. Turn right on San Andreas Drive. Park in the parking area on San Andreas Drive.

For 6000 years, the Miwok Indians had a village at the base of Mount Burdell, which they called Olompali. Food, namely acorns, was abundant, as was water as rains ran down from the ravines. But history changes things. This open space preserve—also once a part of the 8877-acre Olompali Ranch—takes hikers through the green-studded hills, past an old quarry where cobblestone was mined for the streets of San Francisco, and through canyons studded with oaks and bay laurel.

If you're a student of geologic and ecological history, Mount Burdell was created some 12 million years ago when the ocean receded and lava forced its way past the Franciscan sandstone and serpentine. The lava gave way to bunchgrass, where live oak, scrub oak, and bay laurel landed. This oak savanna is typical of the Bay Area.

The preserve now sits wedged among housing developments and a few horse stables. The Marin County Open Space District began buying parcels in 1978 and made the last addition in 1994. The open space now includes 1558 acres of land where mountain bikers, horses, hikers, and dogs are most welcome.

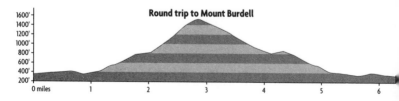

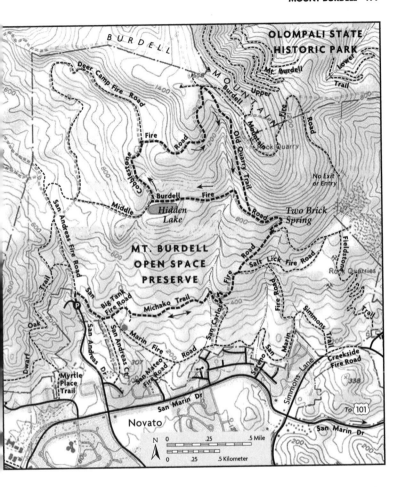

Start at the trailhead on Big Tank Fire Road. At 0.5 mile, turn right onto signed, hiker-only Michako Trail (there's a cattle gate). Continue climbing and, eventually, you'll find yourself on an inviting trail that will snake its way up Mount Burdell's southern shoulder.

At 1.6 miles, head left onto a signed trail past a lone buckeye tree and water troughs, where you may find cows having a drink. Climb to the right and continue on Middle Mount Burdell Fire Road. You'll start to get sweeping views of the surrounding hillsides. The rock quarry appears before the steep climb; carry on to the western knob at 2.9 miles.

To complete the loop portion of the trail, leave the mountain and promptly turn right onto Cobblestone Fire Road. Then turn right off

The rocky summit of Mount Burdell

Cobblestone onto Old Quarry Trail. After 0.5 mile of south-easterly travel, retrace your steps back to the trailhead.

49. Waterfall Trail and Indian Valley

Round trip: 3-mile loop
Hiking time: 1.5 hours
High point: 600 feet
Elevation gain: 500 feet
Best hiking time: September through June
Water: Bring your own
Map: USGS San Rafael
Contact: Marin County Open Space District, (415) 499-6387

Getting there: From US 101, take the Ignacio Boulevard exit that's located a couple of miles south of Highway 37. Go west on Ignacio Boulevard for 2.8 miles and enter the College of Marin campus, where you can park for free at the field house near the softball fields.

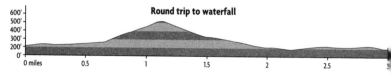

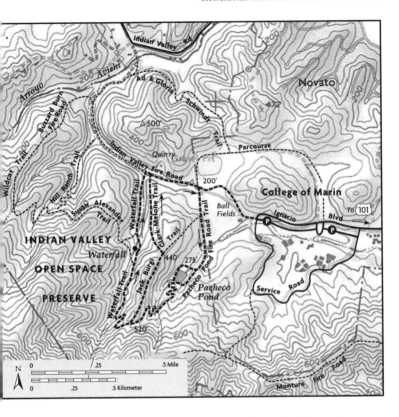

The highlight of this hike is cattail-ringed Pacheco Pond, a quiet space where the dogs will have a wonderful time taking a quick dip—and you can rest and take in a snack. The closeness to the College of Marin makes the Indian Valley Open Space Preserve a popular place on weekends, but the farther back you go on the trails, among the bay laurel and live oak woods, the more solitude you'll seem to find.

The trail begins near left field of the first baseball diamond, which is signed for Pacheco Pond Fire Road Trail. After traveling on this trail for about 150 yards, swing left onto signed Waterfall Trail, where you'll reach circular Pacheco Pond. This 3-acre pond will give your four-footer a chance to swim with the resident duck population.

Back on the trail, a series of switchbacks takes you up the canyon, where shade from the mostly bay laurel forest is a welcome friend. Soaproot (the plant is topped with white flower spikes in June) grows here in clusters, among the seasonal grasses that are tan by summer, only to come alive in greens in the fall.

Pacheco Pond is a great place for dogs to take a swim.

At 1.1 miles, you'll get a great view of San Pablo Bay to the east, and 75 yards farther, you'll reach a three-way trail junction. If taking this trek in the wet months, continue straight on the Waterfall Trail to a slender falls. At any other time, go right and head for the grassy hills to the north.

At 1.6 miles (having headed north), go left onto the signed Clark Melone Trail, which heads down the canyon and reconnects with the Waterfall Trail, where it soon comes to the Indian Valley Fire Road Trail. Turn right here and head straight for the trailhead and a quick, 3-mile loop.

50. Ring Mountain

Round trip: 1.75 miles
Hiking time: 2 hours
High point: 600 feet
Elevation gain: 600 feet
Best hiking time: Year-round
Water: Bring your own
Maps: USGS San Quentin, USGS San Rafael
Contact: Marin County Open Space District, (415) 499-6387

Getting there: From San Francisco, take US 101 north to the Paradise Drive/Tamalpais Drive exit. Turn left off the freeway and make the first right onto San Clemente Drive, which turns into Paradise Drive. Park for free on Paradise Drive, near the wooden gate trailhead and just past the Marin County Day School.

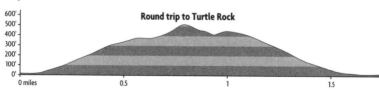

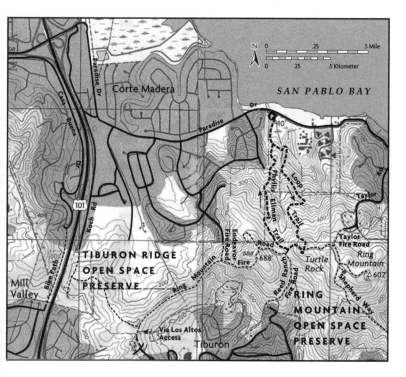

This 377-acre open space preserve encompasses the ridge between the towns of Corte Madera and Tiburon and has great views of San Francisco to the south and the ferries shuttling passengers across San Pablo Bay. It's a surprisingly happy space, one of my favorite hikes in all of the Bay Area.

Besides being an easy hike that gains 600 feet in elevation (so you feel like you've done something when you get to the top), there's a great granite rock outcropping—pack your climbing shoes and chalk bag for a little bouldering while the dogs rest in the shade.

Start at the open space preserve sign and head up the single-track Loop Trail that crosses a bridge at Triangle Marsh; you'll reach a Nature Conservancy sign here that dedicates the area to the memory of Patricia Bucko-Stormer. Before the area was purchased by the Nature Conservancy, development of the surrounding hillsides threatened to consume it. The nonprofit organization, along with the Marin branch of the Native Plant Society, saved the area for everyone's enjoyment. Indeed, this marsh area is home to salt grass, salt pickle weed, poison oak, wildflowers, bay laurel, live oak, and rare plants like the Tiburon mariposa lily, Tiburon paintbrush,

Tiburon buckwheat, Marin dwarf flax, and Oakland star tulip.

Just past the information kiosk that explains the history of the area, take the left trail at the split, through a series of Himalayan blackberry thickets that is the Loop Trail. At marker 4, about 0.3 mile in, you'll reach a criss-cross of trails. Continue right on the main trail; at marker 5, at about 0.5 mile, turn left and pass through a grassland.

At marker 8, you'll reach a shady little grove, where on a railroad tie the word "trail" is etched for everyone to see. At about 0.8 mile, turn right onto unsigned Champe Trail, named after the Nature Conservancy intern who laid out this course. It leads into a forest of bay laurel and, at 1 mile, crosses over the gravel ridge to Turtle Rock.

To get back down, take Ring Mountain Fire Road from Turtle Rock. At 1.5 miles, take the signed Phyllis Ellman Trail and head up the hill and then back down to the trailhead.

51. Blithedale Ridge

Round trip: 7-mile loop
Hiking time: 3–5 hours
High point: 800 feet
Elevation gain: 900 feet
Best hiking time: Year-round
Water: Bring your own
Map: USGS San Rafael
Contact: Marin County Open Space District, (415) 499-6387

Getting there: From US 101 in San Rafael, take the East Blithedale exit a few miles north of the Golden Gate Bridge and go west for 3 miles. Turn right onto West Blithedale Avenue, drive 1.2 miles, and park for free where you can find a spot along the very narrow road near the gate to the Blithedale Summit Open Space Preserve.

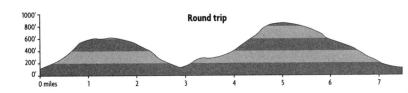

This is a hike where you wouldn't expect it. Nestled in the developments and neighborhoods is a trek that features remote trails through a forest of native trees—mixed hardwood and conifer and some redwoods, too. Six trails lead into this open space, where Dawn Falls is a perfect destination if rains have fallen recently. Best yet, dogs are allowed on all six trails.

Start on the other side of the gate and go up on an old fire road called Two Tanks, which climbs from the trailhead along a babbling stream. Here, you'll be shaded under tan oaks, redwoods, and bigleaf maples. The climb continues after you turn right onto Corte Madera Ridge Road at about 0.8 mile. From here, you'll make a left at Huckleberry Trail, which as the name implies, heads through a thicket of evergreen huckleberries.

Hang another left onto Southern Marin Line Fire Road at 2.1 miles, which is thankfully level for another 2 miles (you'll pass your return route, the Barbara Spring Trail).

A tiny brook greets visitors looking to hike Blithedale Ridge.

Through the peeling madrones, you'll catch some good views. At Dawn Falls Trail, take a right and after a 0.25 mile, reach modest Dawn Falls at 4.3 miles in. The water flows 15 feet down granite slabs peacefully, which is a change of pace from some waterfalls that crash through the brush.

Dawn Falls Trail continues along a deeply shaded canyon to the Barbara Spring Trail, where you'll make a right, then turn right again to retrace a part of Marin Line Road before making a left onto a connector trail that links up to Corte Madera Ridge Road. Make a left at Corte Madera Ridge Road, then a right, which will take you back to the gate on Two Tanks Road.

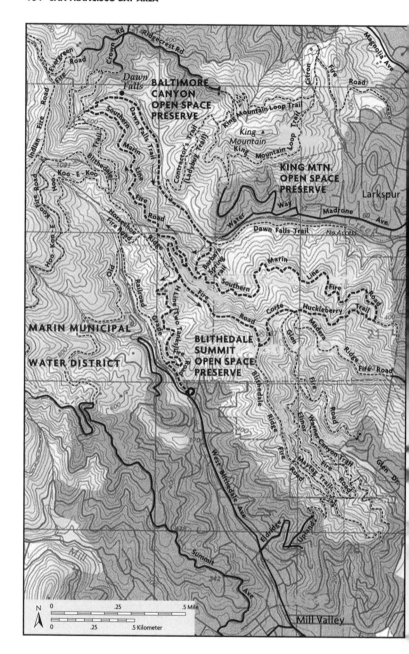

52. Rodeo Lagoon

Round trip: 1.7 miles
Hiking time: 1 hour
High point: 170 feet
Elevation gain: 170 feet
Best hiking time: Year-round
Water: At the trailhead
Map: USGS Point Bonita
Contact: Golden Gate National Recreation Area, Marin Headlands
Visitor Center, (415) 331-1540

Getting there: From just north of the Golden Gate Bridge on US 101, take the Alexander Avenue exit and turn immediately left under the freeway. Follow the brown recreation signs for Marin Headlands and drive the twisty road (which has great views of the Golden Gate and San Francisco) about 2 miles, where you'll end up on Bunker Road. Park for free in the large lot at Fort Barry.

Getting here is half the fun. The Marin Headlands is 15 square miles of beaches, marshes, lagoons, and lush coastal hills that rise to spectacular views.

Wildlife lovers will love this trek, since there's the chance to spot a number of raptor species, seabirds, marine mammals, and the occasional bobcat and mountain lion. History buffs will be pumped about the 150 years of military history, including bunkers, batteries, cannons, and in an extension of this hike, a trek past on old Nike missile site. Dog lovers love it, well, because it's a place where leashed dogs can stroll, too.

From the Civil War through the Cold War, the Marin Headlands—along with the Presidio across the Golden Gate Bridge—protected San Francisco Bay from invasion. The Marin Headlands served as a military base until the 1960s; now it hosts a network of mixed-use trails. This trip

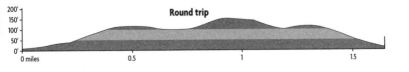

alongside Rodeo Lagoon is an easy warm-up for the nearby 6.6-mile Miwok and Bobcat Trails (Hike 53).

The hike's starting point, Fort Barry, was once a major post for military operations. After walking around the fort, cross the road and go up the hill to the trailhead. First, you'll head out toward a bluff overlook, where you'll catch surfers catching waves on Rodeo Beach.

Then, you'll take the trail that hugs the south side of Rodeo Lagoon. The lagoon is a mixed freshwater/saltwater area that rises and falls with the seasons. Swelled by rainwater, the lagoon stays mostly brackish-brown, but make no mistake about it, the waterway is teeming with life. In fall, the endangered brown pelican is present, along with egrets, ducks, gulls, and herons.

It's easy to extend this hike to up to 4.5 miles, making a loop from the south side of the lagoon around the Nike missile site (now in a state of disrepair) and along Rodeo Beach.

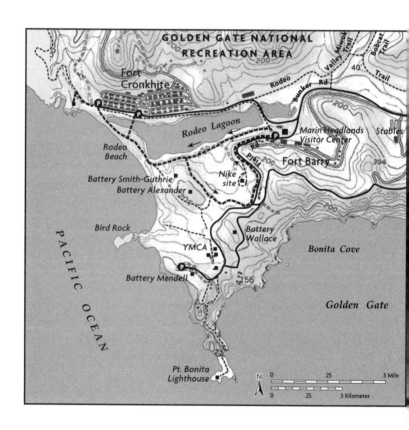

Rodeo Lagoon is a great place to spot a variety of bird species.

53. Miwok and Bobcat Trails

Round trip: 6.6-mile loop
Hiking time: 2–3 hours
High point: 1050 feet
Elevation gain: 1250 feet
Best hiking time: Year-round
Water: At the trailhead
Map: USGS Point Bonita
Contact: Golden Gate National Recreation Area, Marin Headlands Visitor Center (415) 331-1540 Check regarding the latest on regulations on where dogs can be walked.

Getting there: From just north of the Golden Gate Bridge on US 101, take the Alexander Avenue exit and turn immediately left under the freeway. Follow the brown recreation signs for Marin Headlands and drive the twisty road (which has great views of the Golden Gate and San Francisco) about 2 miles and park for free in the large lot on the north side of Rodeo Lagoon.

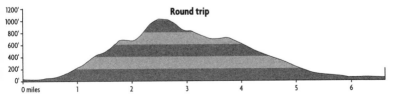

This nearly circular trail takes hikers along a wide path up and down the pretty grasslands that make up the Marin Headlands. It's hard to imagine that for nearly 100 years, the area served as a military base of operations. In spring, the grassy hills are filled with wildflowers, including purplish-blue lupine and creamsicle-orange California poppies.

The Miwok and Bobcat Trails will escort you around the U-shaped Gerbode Valley, which takes on many facets during the year. Windswept grassy hills show their colors in spring with the aforementioned wild-flower display, go brown in the summer heat, and when the clouds and fog descend, it's eerie and mysterious.

It's easy to extend this trek by using a number of connector trails (pick up a copy of the free Marin Headlands brochure from the visitor center),

The Miwok Trail is wide and inviting.

but this loop provides a decent workout for hikers and their canine friends. It also gets pretty solitary, and hikers will have a chance to see coyotes, bobcats, and even mountain lions (when we were last there, signs at the trailhead warned of sightings).

One note: as this is a national recreation area, the rangers are sticklers about dogs being on a leash at all times. Let's keep our dog-friendly spaces open and obey the rules. Also, this trek is used heavily by Bay Area horse enthusiasts, so be warned—you and your pooch will likely run into a few horseback riders.

The hike starts at Rodeo Lagoon, where you'll head northeast on the signed Miwok Trail. The trail follows a creek for a bit, then starts to climb up Wolf Ridge. Stay on the Miwok Trail and you'll reach a gap at 1.2 miles, where there's a trail junction. Go right and right again at the next junction.

Here's where the climbing comes in on this hike, as you ascend to the trek's high point just prior to reaching the Bobcat Trail turnoff and a gentle downhill. The views—when the clouds and fog are gone—are inspiring, with the Tennessee Valley to the northwest and the Gerbode Valley to the southeast.

Go right on the Bobcat Trail at 3.3 miles. Backpackers (backcountry permit required) can turn right at 4 miles to camp at Hawk Camp, but dog walkers will want to continue on the Bobcat Trail and take another right turn at 4.3 miles, where you'll drop steadily into the valley.

At 6.3 miles, turn right onto the signed Rodeo Valley Trail. Then take an immediate left back onto the Miwok Trail and return to the parking area.

54. Fort Baker

Round trip: 2.5 miles
Hiking time: 2 hours
High point: 600 feet
Elevation gain: 600 feet
Best hiking time: Year-round
Water: Bring your own
Map: USGS San Francisco North
Contact: Golden Gate National Recreation Area, Marin Headlands
Visitor Center, (415) 331-1540

Getting there: From San Francisco, drive north on US 101 and cross the Golden Gate Bridge, get in the right lane and take the Vista Point exit to the Vista Point parking lot.

This hike is a quiet secret: a nifty drop from Vista Point on the north side of the Golden Gate Bridge to Fort Baker below. And completing the hike depends on the country's present threat level.

See, once the Office of Homeland Security's threat level goes to orange, this trail is off-limits to hikers. But in that case you'll either have the option of crossing the Golden Gate—possibly the Bay Area's most frequented stroll—or of driving down to Fort Baker to wander among the historic buildings, as well as taking in the shoreline and maybe striking up a conversation with the U.S. Coast Guard crews stationed there.

Vista Point is like a mini United Nations, where people from across the globe come to gaze at the famous brick-red bridge and the San Francisco skyline. They stop to take pictures, maybe cross the bridge—you can go halfway to admire the view, turn back to the car, and you've gone 1.5 miles—but most people never think to take the short walk down to Fort Baker. A paved trail from the parking area loops under the northern footings of the Golden Gate, then works its way back around to the fort.

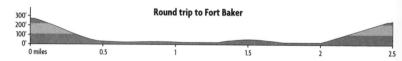

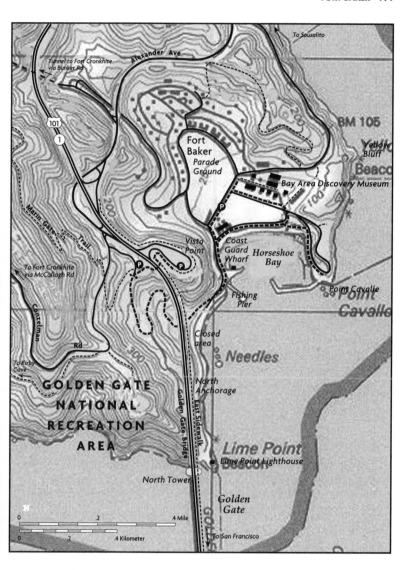

The U.S. Army established Fort Baker in 1897 to support the many coastal batteries that were established on the northern side of the Golden Gate. According to Golden Gate National Recreational Area information, Fort Baker was a departure from earlier, western military forts. It represented a new, modern army, one where enlisted men and officers enjoyed a better standard of living.

Once you wind your way to the base of the Golden Gate (be sure to

The Golden Gate Bridge and the Pacific Coast were protected from invasion at Fort Baker.

bring a camera for probably the best views of the bridge and the San Francisco skyline), take the road along the shore toward the Bay Area Discovery Museum (interesting displays; no dogs allowed). From a kiosk in the museum's main parking area, be sure to pick up the brochure for the new self-guided Fort Baker History Walk, and amble the 0.5-mile trail that makes nine stops through the fort. Dogs are welcome to come along, as long as they're leashed.

Once you've completed the loop, head out toward Horseshoe Bay to take in the salt breezes and see how the shore fishermen are doing. Then return to the north footing of the bridge and the moderately strenuous walk back up to the parking area.

55. Golden Gate Promenade

Round trip: 6 miles
Hiking time: 2–3 hours
High point: 175 feet
Elevation gain: 150 feet
Best hiking time: Year-round
Water: Best to bring your own
Map: USGS San Francisco North
Contact: Golden Gate National Recreation Area, (415) 331-1540

Getting there: From US 101 on the south side of the Golden Gate Bridge, take the Marina Boulevard exit and head south toward Fisherman's

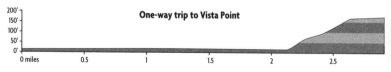

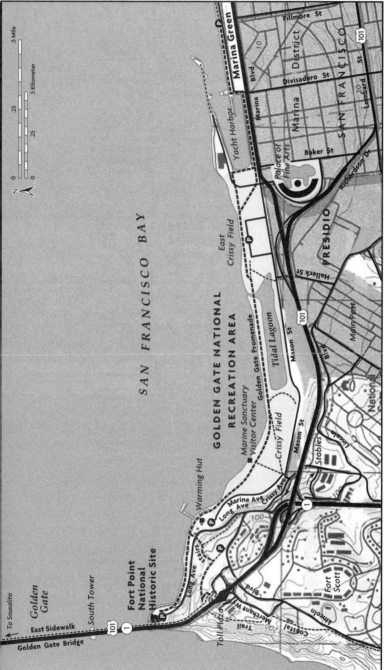

The Golden Gate Promenade is popular with nearly everyone.

Wharf. Parking lots are available off Marina Boulevard at Fort Mason, Marina Green, Crissy Field, and near the St. Francis Yacht Club. The route below begins at Marina Green.

OK, OK, this trek leads you past a lot of what people come to San Francisco for in the first place. But hey, who says we can't be hikers *and* sightseers?

This paved trail heads along the shoreline of San Francisco Bay from Marina Green to Fort Point and the southern footings of the Golden Gate Bridge. Along the way, you'll see the sights, like the San Francisco skyline, Alcatraz, Tiburon, San Francisco Bay, and of course, the brick-red bridge that just might be the most photographed landmark in the Bay Area—the Golden Gate.

This is a leisurely hike where you can socialize with other dog lovers (be sure to ask before introducing your pooch to other leashed pets) and people-watch to your heart's content. Plan on gusty, cool breezes come afternoon and bring a jacket—Mark Twain wasn't kidding when he said, "The coldest winter I ever spent was a summer in San Francisco."

The entire length of the promenade is hip and artsy. In the morning, and again in the evening, recreational joggers fill the trail, and during the day you'll pass people painting, playing drums, or making sand sculptures, and others who will likely be fishing, in-line skating, and riding mountain bikes.

After passing Marina Green, a large grassy area where you'll likely see fanciful kite fliers, head toward Crissy Field, where the first aircraft to this field landed in preparation for coastal defense in the 1920s. Soon, you'll reach Fort Point, where the U.S. Army seeded the bay around the Golden Gate with mines in World War II.

After a short climb through a garden setting, Battery East comes into view, where five gigantic guns once protected the bay entrance, way back in 1870. Go through the tunnel and look down on Fort Point proper, where the red-brick buildings were designed to mount 126 huge muzzle-loaded cannons (but nary a one was actually fired).

Continue on underneath the Golden Gate, hang out, then reverse your tracks to head back to Marina Green and the maze of people doing their things.

56. Sweeney Ridge

Round trip: 4.2 miles
Hiking time: 3 hours
High point: 1250 feet
Elevation gain: 550 feet
Best hiking time: Year-round; streams might not be passable in early spring
Water: From Boulder Creek
Map: USGS San Francisco South
Contact: Golden Gate National Recreation Area, (415) 561-4700

Getting there: From the San Francisco Bay Bridge, take US 101 south to Interstate 280 south. Take the Pacifica/Highway 1 exit and then get off at Skyline Boulevard south, signed for Highway 35. Past the Skyline College entrance, about 4 miles, turn right on Sneath Lane and drive it through the neighborhood until its end. The parking area is on the right past the gate.

I don't live in the Bay Area; if I did, I'd take the dogs on this hike as many times as I could.

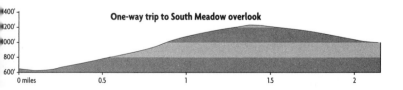

One-way trip to South Meadow overlook

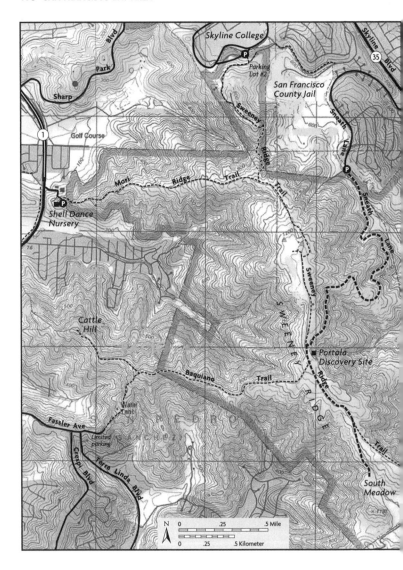

Sweeney Ridge is the dividing point between Pacifica and San Bruno, about 10 miles south of San Francisco proper. As a hiker (and outdoor writer–type) said about this trek, "No matter how long you've lived in the Bay Area, there's always a chance to make it new again."

The ridge, which includes the busy I-280/US 101 corridor and San Francisco International Airport, rises 1250 feet above the din, offering 360-degree views and something much better—some solitude from the

The view from atop Sweeney Ridge, where wildlife abounds in an urban setting.

very urban setting below. Protected as part of the Golden Gate National Recreation Area in 1984, there are trails here that will help you leave civilization, if only for a little while.

This hike starts with 550 feet of climbing, which isn't all bad, especially if the dogs have been in the car for any length of time. The views start on your left as you climb, with San Andreas Lake coming into focus, then Crystal Springs. While there are four access points total to this area, this trek brings you up the ridge directly to the Portola Discovery Site.

In 1769, an expedition led by Don Gaspar de Portola was charged with finding an overland route to Monterey Bay. The Spanish party left Mexico with sixty-four men and 200 horses, including one scout, Jose Francisco Ortega. Ortega climbed the ridge near the group's camp (in the Linda Mar area of Pacifica today) and said he saw "an enormous area of the sea, or estuary, which shot inland as far as the eye could see." He became the first European to see San Francisco Bay.

On the ridge, you'll stand directly on that historic spot, now dedicated with a monument to Carl McCarthy, who helped secure public ownership of the area. The views here are just stunning, with the Bay Area and San Pedro Mountain, Montara Mountain, Mori Ridge, the Crystal Springs watershed, Mount Diablo, and the Mount Hamilton range.

It's easy to stop here, but walk a little farther, just 10 minutes. As you continue south on the ridge, look for a side trail off to the right (it's not signed). Make the right, and in 5 minutes, you'll arrive at an overlook of what is known as South Meadow—a fantastic wildlife habitat where deer, rabbits, quail, and raptors make their home—along with a stunning view of the ocean.

Once you've had your fill, reverse course back to your car, back to humanity.

57. Fort Funston Sunset Trail

Round trip: 1.5-mile loop
Hiking time: 1 hour
High point: 180 feet
Elevation gain: Negligible
Best hiking time: Fall and winter (to avoid heavy fog); hikable year-round
Water: From fountains
Map: USGS San Francisco South
Contact: Fort Funston Ranger Station, (415) 239-2366

Getting there: From near Daly City, take Interstate 280 to Highway 1 in San Bruno. Turn west and drive 1 mile to Highway 35/Skyline Boulevard. Turn right (north) onto Highway 35 and drive 5 miles, where you'll bear left and pass Lake Merced. Turn left at Fort Funston and park for free. From San Francisco, take Geary Boulevard west until it dead-ends at the ocean near the Cliff House Restaurant. Turn left onto the Great Highway and drive 4 miles to the parking area.

If they built an amusement park just for dogs, it would look like Fort Funston. I mean, this Golden Gate Recreation Area park puts the fun in Funston. Dog owners are actually encouraged to take their dogs off-leash for frolicking with the seemingly hundreds of other dogs that scamper along the park's paved Sunset Trail. There are plenty of places to stop and sniff, areas to chase balls, and plenty of warm sand to roll in.

The Fort Funston Dog Walkers promote good stewardship of the area (as well as assuring that the area stays dog-friendly) by providing plastic bags to police your pooch, as well as policing the area themselves.

Here, you'll also see people hang gliding off the cliff (there's a launching area just south of the parking area), as well as history buffs who come

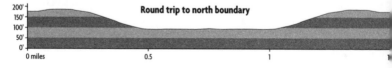

to visit the remnants of Battery Richmond P. Davis, which was completed in the early 1900s. The battery, which included two state-of-the-art 16-inch guns that each had a range of 25 miles, featured 10 feet of reinforced concrete topped by 20 feet of earth, which made it nearly impossible to see from the air. The battery was dismantled in 1948, but you can still wander around the fortified concrete structure.

This trail is best in fall and winter, when the fog clears and a walk at dusk will bring goosebumps—not from the chilled Pacific air, but from the sight of the sun sinking into the ocean.

Pick up the Sunset Trail near the viewing area for the hang gliders and go north. It meanders through the coastal bluffs (signs warn against getting too close) for 0.75 mile to the park's boundary. Then you can loop back around to your car.

You can also drop down to Ocean Beach (Hike 58), where you'll likely see a variety of dog breeds happily chasing balls and retrieving driftwood

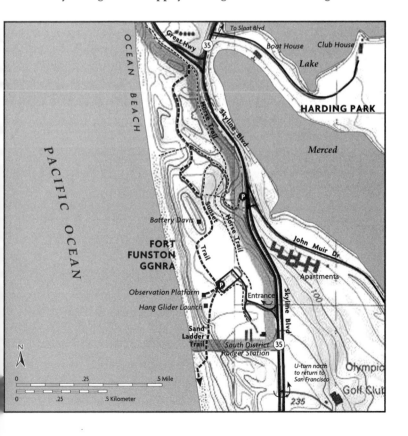

Signs warn hikers and dogs not to stray too close to the crumbly cliff.

from the surf. To get to the beach, walk south from the parking area and look for the Sand Ladder Trail toward the edge of the bluff.

58. Ocean Beach Esplanade

Round trip: 6 miles
Hiking time: 3 hours
High point: 150 feet
Elevation gain: 150 feet
Best hiking time: Fall and winter (to avoid heavy fog); hikable year-round
Water: From fountains, but bring some of your own
Map: USGS San Francisco South
Contact: Fort Funston Ranger Station, (415) 239- 2366

Getting there: From near Daly City, take Interstate 280 to Highway 1 in San Bruno. Turn west and drive 1 mile to Highway 35/Skyline Boulevard. Turn right (north) onto Highway 35 and drive 5 miles, where you'll bear

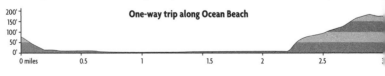

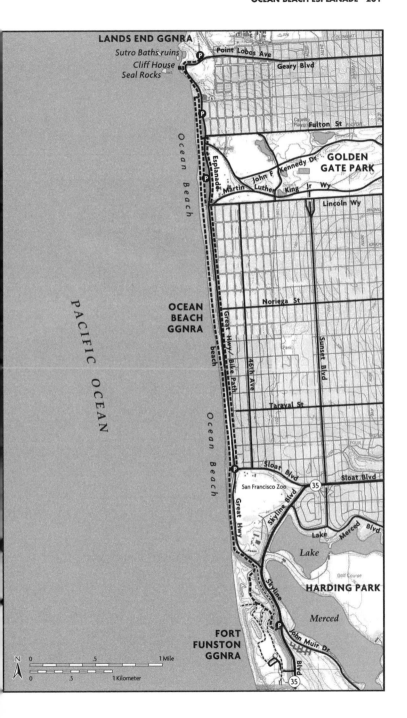

The Ocean Beach Esplanade is wide, inviting and cooled by sea breezes.

left and pass Lake Merced. Turn left at Fort Funston and park for free. Alternately, from San Francisco, take Geary Boulevard west until it dead-ends at the ocean near the Cliff House Restaurant. Turn left onto the Great Highway and drive 1 mile to the parking area.

This expanse of beach is popular with many a group, from surfers who tackle the rough surf (the undertow here is tremendous; swimming is not allowed in the frigid waters), to runners passing over the hard-packed sand when the tide is low, to dogs and their owners out for a little exercise.

Ocean Beach features sand, surf, a paved trail, and the chance to explore Fort Funston (Hike 57) and Thornton Beach. Since there's the option of a paved trail, as well as the sandy expanse, you can create treks of variable length. The beach stretches from Seal Rocks near the Cliff House south to Fort Funston.

On the paved trail, please leash your dog and keep strict control, as this is a popular stop for tourists as well as locals. You used to be able to take your dog off-leash on the beach, but no more. The rangers and park police are enforcing the leash law on Ocean Beach.

Amble along the beach to the Esplanade's terminus at Fort Funston and watch people beachcombing for shells and bits of glass polished by wave action.

59. Rockaway Point

Round trip: 2.6 miles
Hiking time: 1–2 hours
High point: 150 feet
Elevation gain: 150 feet
Best hiking time: Year-round
Water: Bring your own
Map: USGS Montara Mountain
Contact: Pacifica Parks Division, (650) 738-7380

Getting there: Drive to the south end of the community of Pacifica on Highway 1 and park for free in the large paved lot signed for San Pedro Beach, about a block north of Linda Mar Boulevard.

The first thing you'll notice on this hike is how many people pack the middle of Pacifica State Beach; but walk all the way to Rockaway Point and there's a chance you'll have the spot to yourself.

The beach, just behind the new Taco Bell restaurant, is popular with surfers who'll jam the area to check out the waves. But those knowledgeable in Pacifica seek out the block-shaped Rockaway Point—it's said to hum with magical vibrations—where you'll get a good look at the ocean from the easily climbable surface.

Start this hike from the parking lot and head north. This stretch of beach features hard-packed cocoa-colored sand, and if your dogs are like mine, they'll chase the frothy white surf—then run from the next incoming wave. San Pedro Beach is nearly level, and where the low sand dunes rise to meet the sprawl near Highway 1, ice plants bloom is a variety of colors in the spring.

Be sure to look to the southeast at Montara Mountain, which is shrouded by cloud cover for much of the year. There are a few Monterey cypress here, but they don't grow as magnificent as in some coastal areas due to the pounding the area gets from the brisk sea breezes.

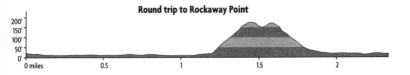

Round trip to Rockaway Point

You'll reach the bluff of Rockaway Point in a little under a mile, where you'll get the best view of San Pedro Rock, which rises from the sea like volcanic lumps. Here, you'll find your first spur trail that will cross a gulch and lead into an area of sea stacks, where you can explore at low tide. Go a bit farther, about halfway around Rockaway Point, for great views of the impressive sea stacks, which seem to frame Montara Mountain.

From here, retrace your steps to the northern edge of the beach at about 1.2 miles and find another trail that leads up Rockaway Point. The summit is actually a sloping field that allows for exploration and fantastic, 360-degree views of the area. Come in the spring, and the area will be ablaze in wildflowers.

Once you're finished exploring, just retrace your steps back to your car.

The view toward Point San Pedro along the Pacific Coast

60. Gray Whale Cove

Round trip: 4 miles
Hiking time: 2 hours
High point: 100 feet
Elevation gain: 150 feet
Best hiking time: Year-round
Water: Bring your own
Map: USGS Montara Mountain
Contact: Pacifica Parks Division, (650) 738-7380

Getting there: Drive south on Highway 1 past the community of Pacifica to just north of Montara State Beach, some 10 miles north of Half Moon Bay. There's an unsigned gate on the east side of the highway where you can park for free; if it's packed with surfers heading to the beach, you can also access the trail from the free parking area at Montara State Beach.

This hike takes in the rugged Pacific coastline, where every view becomes a study of how the surf pounds the land. While the waves crash, you'll be pleasantly above it all, where the views give you a feeling of being

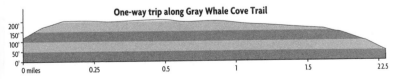

One-way trip along Gray Whale Cove Trail

perched on a lookout of a sailing ship—the wind constantly in your face. The trail stays near winding Highway 1, but it never seems to detract from the view. Don't forget to bring your camera, as there are plenty of chances to take new and better shots of the sand, surf, and cliffs.

One note of caution: if you opt to take the wooden stairs down to Gray Whale Cove, the beach is clothing-optional. Gawkers are not welcome here, so stay on the trail to get arguably better views.

Gray Whale Cove Trail is mostly flat and, through its numerous twists and turns, you'll likely see waves of coffeeberry, monkey flower, and lizard's tail shrubs and coyote brush. A spur trail at 1.3 miles climbs steeply for some 200 yards to a welcoming knoll that offers great views of Montara Mountain and the blue Pacific.

Back on the main trail, you'll drop gently for a bit to another parking area, which signals the point where you'll turn back to your own vehicle.

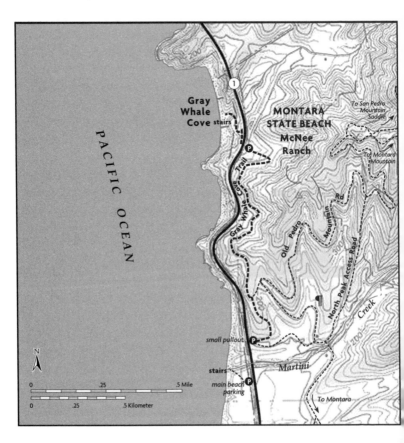

61. San Pedro Mountain

Round trip: 6 miles
Hiking time: 3 hours
High point: 1840 feet
Elevation gain: 1740 feet
Best hiking time: Year-round
Water: Bring your own
Map: USGS Montara Mountain
Contact: McNee Ranch State Park Ranger Office, (650) 726-8819;
   Half Moon Bay State Parks, (650) 726-8820

Getting there: From San Francisco, take Highway 1 south 17 miles through Pacifica. Continue south, past Devils Slide and down to the base of the hill. Look for a small pullout on the left. The trail access point is at a yellow gate with a state park property sign on it; do not block the gate. If the area is full, try parking at the lot on the west side of Highway 1 at Montara State Beach.

I'll admit it: I have a sick fascination with peak bagging. It's not my fault, you see. I have a border collie and it's the only way I can get her to behave in the car. Tire her out so she'll actually sleep on the way home.

On this hike, you'll gain 1740 feet in a very short stretch. This trail actually started in 1879, when settlers of Pacifica pushed a dirt trail up from the coastline over San Pedro Mountain, according to the city of Pacifica. Other than peak baggers, this hike is for people who love a challenge, with a great payoff of spectacular views.

One note of caution: fog and wind pound the area at certain times of the year, so get a dependable weather report before venturing out and always pack raingear, just in case.

To start, go past the yellow gate and bear left through the coastal grasslands on an old fire road. The first few steps really don't inspire (you'll hear constant traffic noise from Highway 1), but stick with it. As you continue and rise to the first ridge, you'll be able to see how the trail tracks up the

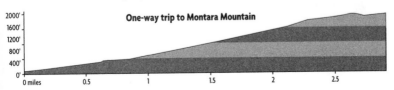

One-way trip to Montara Mountain

Wildflowers on the way up to San Pedro Ridge

spine of this coastal mountain. Sure, it's a brutal grade, but you'll be pleased with yourself for reaching the top.

The trail cuts through plenty of coffeeberry and poison oak, so be sure to stay on the trail. You'll likely to be passed by plenty of mountain bikers, so also make sure you keep your dog leashed, lest you cause an accident.

Once you top out, you'll have spectacular views of the ocean, Mount Diablo, Sweeney Ridge (Hike 56), and the San Francisco Bay. After you've had your fill of the views—and you've filled the tanks with some water and snacks—it's time to head back down the old fire road to your car.

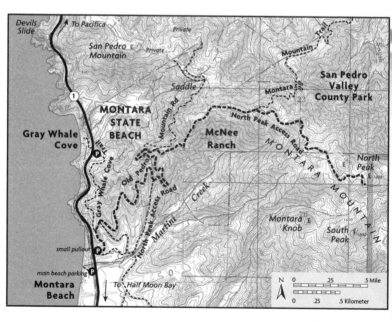

62. Pulgas Ridge

Round trip: 2.5-mile loop
Hiking time: 1.5 hours
High point: 670 feet
Elevation gain: 400 feet
Best hiking time: September through June; hikable year-round
Water: Bring your own
Map: From Midpeninsula Regional Open Space District online
Contact: Midpeninsula Regional Open Space District, San Mateo
County, (650) 691-1200, www.openspace.org

Getting there: From Interstate 280 in San Mateo County, take the Edgewood exit and drive 1 mile east, then turn left onto Crestview Drive (just before the entrance to Edgewood Park). Almost immediately, take a left onto Edmonds Road. After just 0.1 mile, park on the right side of the road, near the gated entrance to the Redwood Center.

In the Bay Area, you'll hear a lot of rants about this 293-acre preserve. This former tuberculosis sanitarium owned by the city of San Francisco was transformed into an open space preserve in 1983 and the buildings were torn down in 1985.

The squawking comes from people who don't care for dogs. See, Pulgas Ridge has a huge open space where dogs are allowed to be off-leash (meanwhile, mountain bikers and horses aren't allowed in the preserve, which is another story). Trouble is, many people have adopted this off-leash policy for the trails, and that is against the rules. Stay out of the fray by putting your pooch on the leash, since it's a short, 1.5-mile level hike to the dog-friendly open space.

The Pulgas Ridge Open Space Preserve is a well-maintained, quaint little park where you'll get to schmooze with other dog owners. Currently, there are four trails in the preserve; the Midpeninsula Regional Open Space District has promised to complete more in the next few years.

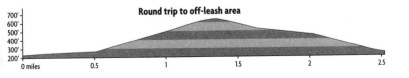

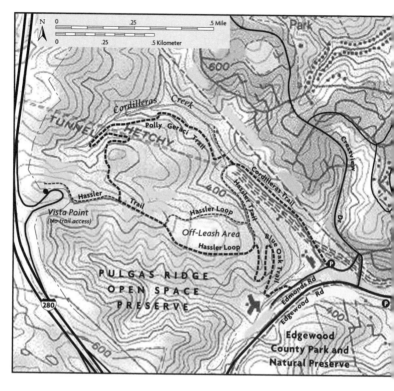

Start this trek—signed the Cordilleras Trail—at the kiosk. It cuts through private land, so stay on the trail. After 0.4 mile, at a signed junction, continue uphill on Cordilleras Trail. After just a few feet, you'll pick up the Polly Geraci Trail, where you'll turn left. In the spring, this area of trail is alive with ferns, poison oak, Indian warrior, milkmaids, and columbine. You'll likely see and hear deer crashing through the underbrush, under a canopy of buckeye, coast live oak, bay laurel, and madrone.

At 1.4 miles, the trail ends at a signed junction with the Hassler Trail. Here, you'll make a left and enter a thicket of eucalyptus. This paved trail heads downhill and, in good weather, offers the best views toward the Santa Cruz Mountains.

Ferns abound in spring along Polly Geraci Trail.

The trail splits at the off-leash area at 1.5 miles. Be sure to see who is hanging out, and bring a Frisbee or ball to share.

Back on the trail, bear right at the split to enjoy better views on your way back to the entrance. At 1.9 miles, you'll hit the Blue Oak Trail, which runs out at 2.3 miles, where the trail puts you back on Edmonds Road. Turn left and walk back to the trailhead.

63. Arastradero Preserve

Round trip: 3.8-mile loop
Hiking time: 2–3 hours
High point: 650 feet
Elevation gain: 400 feet
Best hiking time: Year-round
Water: From spigot in the parking area
Map: USGS Palo Alto
Contact: City of Palo Alto, (650) 329-2423

Getting there: From Interstate 280 in Santa Clara County, exit at Page Mill Road and drive west about 0.3 mile. Turn right onto Arastradero Road, continue about 0.5 mile, and turn right into the parking lot.

Rolling grasslands, oak savannas, and a pretty little lake that's got fish in it. This little slice of heaven is comparatively underused by most busy Bay Area residents. But that doesn't mean you should skip the Arastradero Preserve. No sir. The trails are mostly flat and wide and can accommodate mountain bikers, horse riders, hikers, and dog walkers. The destination here is Arastradero Lake, a little man-made lake that has all the charm of its natural cousins.

From the parking lot, you'll strike out on the signed Gateway Trail, where at less than 0.25 mile, you'll cross Arastradero Road and be in the preserve proper on the Juan Bautista de Anza Trail. Watch for quail, deer, bobcats, and coyote. Besides the abundance of poison oak, also look for wild rose

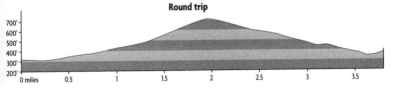

(the blooms are fantastic in the fall), willow, coast live oak, monkey flower, snowberry, and blackberry (which make for great snacking in the spring).

The trail crosses a creek at a bridge, then meets up with signed Meadowlark Trail at about 0.4 mile. Here, the trail climbs slightly, then dips down toward the lake. In spring, the hills closer to the lake will be covered with California poppy, as well as buttercup, lupine, bluedicks, and tomcat clover. Just before 0.6 mile at a signed junction, a bridge leads left just before the lake, but stay straight. About 0.1 mile farther on, bear left at a signed junction (where the pump house stands) and you'll find yourself on Arastradero Creek Trail.

Along this trail, there are a few spots where you can get to the water's edge, but watch out for all the poison oak. Fishing is open on the lake year-round, and all state Department of Fish and Game rules apply. There is no swimming here.

At 0.7 mile, you'll come to another spur, but continue straight along Arastradero Creek; you'll notice that the trail parallels the creek, but the water is blocked by a thicket of vegetation. At 1.3 miles, the trail reaches the Woodrat Trail; turn right. The route climbs through

The Arastradero Preserve is a mix of grasslands and oak.

the grasslands, making an easy zigzag through the stands of poison oak. At 1.7 miles, you'll reach a T junction, where you'll turn left. At 1.8 miles, come to another T junction, where you'll turn right to get back on the Meadowlark Trail. Be sure to take a gander at the giant valley oaks here, which make for a stark photograph at sunset.

At almost 2 miles, you'll reach the signed junction for the Vista Point Trail, where you'll bear left. This trail passes a picnic area in a grove of olive trees, and makes for a nice stop about 0.1 mile from the junction. After a break, retrace your steps to the junction and take a left onto the Meadowlark Trail, which descends toward the Juan Bautista de Anza Trail and the parking area.

64. Anthony Chabot Loop

Round trip: 8.6-mile loop
Hiking time: 3–5 hours
High point: 500 feet
Elevation gain: 500 feet
Best hiking time: Year-round
Water: At the trailhead
Map: USGS Las Trampas Ridge
Contact: East Bay Regional Park District, (510) 635-0135

Getting there: From Interstate 580 just south of Oakland, take the Estudillo Avenue exit and go east for 0.2 mile. Turn right onto Lake Chabot Road,

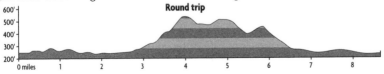

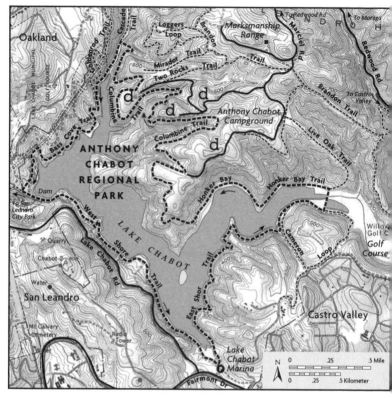

drive 2.6 miles, and park for free on the road just before the turnoff to the marina. You can pay to park inside the park. Also note that it's $1 to bring your dog in (but the nice ranger will give your pooch a treat).

This trek takes you along the hidden bays and coves of 315-acre Lake Chabot; plenty of stairways lead to the water's edge where you can cast a line or just admire the view. This area was closed to visitors for ninety-one years, after the lake was completed in 1875. Then, on one weekend in 1966, the lake opened to some 30,000 anglers eager to cast a line in the still blue waters (the lake has bass, trout, crappie, bluegill, and carp).

This 5065-acre park is an open space among the development of Oakland and San Leandro. You'll pass the busy marina, where anglers in rented boats and people looking for a little pleasure paddle out for a cruise. Indeed, for both the first and last mile, you'll run into crowds of people, bicyclists, anglers, joggers, and families pushing strollers. But the more you hike, the fewer people you'll see. Lake Chabot also currently serves

Views abound along the Anthony Chabot Loop.

as an emergency water supply, so you and you dog will be asked to observe certain regulations about jumping in (swimming isn't allowed).

You'll begin on the paved East Shore Trail, which takes you past the aforementioned staircases. The vegetation here is a mixed salad, with poppy and wild radish in the spring and cow parsnips and creambush later on. This is a pleasant, level stroll, under the cover of bay laurel and oak. At 1.9 miles, you'll reach the tip of Honker Bay, where you'll cross a small footbridge and come to an area that's free of cover. Soon, you'll enter a eucalyptus grove, as the Honker Bay Trail hugs the shoreline.

At 3.4 miles, bear left at a junction and head to the Anthony Chabot Campground (Chabot was a pioneering businessman who created Lake Chabot by constructing an earthen dam in 1874–75). You'll climb from the lake into the surrounding forest on the Columbine Trail. This is the most isolated part of the trek, which crosses canyons where seasonal streams burble with water in the winter.

Turn left at the signed Bass Cove Trail at 4.8 miles. It'll take you south and past an area where ducks and geese squawk incessantly. You'll find fantastic views of the lake here, framed by bay laurel, buckeye, and coast live oak.

At 6.8 miles, you'll turn left onto the paved West Shore Trail where you'll spend the next 2 miles in shaded comfort on this level path. The trail leads past the marina and into the parking area.

65. Bort Meadow

Round trip: 5.4-mile loop
Hiking time: 3 hours
High point: 1200 feet
Elevation gain: 1000 feet
Best hiking time: September through June; hikable year-round
Water: Bring plenty of your own
Map: USGS Las Trampas Ridge
Contact: East Bay Regional Park District, (510) 562-7275

Getting there: From Highway 24 in Alameda County, exit Highway 13 south. Drive about 4 miles and exit at Redwood Road. Turn left onto Redwood and drive uphill about 0.5 mile to the junction with Skyline Boulevard. Stay in the left lane, and continue straight on Redwood about 4.3 miles to the trailhead on the right side of the road.

From westbound Interstate 580 in Alameda County, take the Castro Valley exit to Castro Valley Boulevard. Turn left on Castro Valley Boulevard, then right on Redwood Road. Drive north about 6 miles to the trailhead on the left side of the road.

It's hard to imagine that a place so wild and so rugged exists so close to the hustle and bustle of downtown Oakland. But Bort Meadow is a magical place where you can pretend you're a Wild West settler seeking fame and fortune.

This hike features a lush grassland ringed by redwoods and eucalyptus, where you're bound to see an abundance of wildlife, including quail, bobcat, deer, coyote, and a number of raptors circling above. This hike can get very hot in the summer, so it's best to stick to visits from September through June. In spring, you'll have the chance to walk through an expanse of wildflowers.

Start by descending a paved road from the Bort Meadow Staging Area,

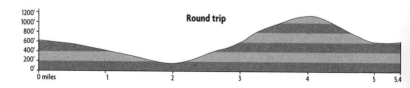

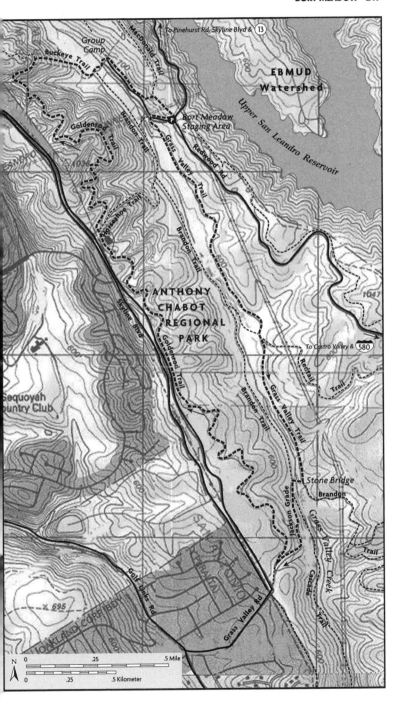

where at 0.1 miles, you'll come to a sign that announces three trails. Take the left trail, onto the Grass Valley Trail. This multiuse trail (be sure to yield to the frequent mountain bikers and horses) is nearly flat and somewhat curvy. This is actually part of the East Bay Skyline National Recreation Trail, as well as the Bay Area Ridge Trail.

At just over 1 mile, you'll reach a signed junction, where Redtail Trail bears left. Stay on the Grass Valley Trail as this dirt path winds downhill and the grasslands give way to towering groves of eucalyptus and even taller redwoods. At 1.5 miles, the trail reaches a stone bridge, where you'll want to go left and uphill. Turn right and cross Grass Valley Creek (a good water stop for the dogs when it's flowing), and pass the signed Cascade Trail to the left and start hoofing it up Jackson Grade.

This old fire road offers some shaded relief, and after a short climb to the ridgeline it ends. Pick up the signed Goldenrod Trail and continue climbing. The trail actually nears Skyline Boulevard and stays close to the road, where you'll first gaze out at the buildings of the equestrian center at 3.6 miles. Turn left to stay on the Goldenrod Trail, just before the gated trail crosses into the equestrian center (if the vegetation is tall, it might make it hard to see the signpost).

At 3.75 miles, the trail leads right toward the Horseshoe Trail, which drops down to the valley and meets up with the Brandon Trail. But you'll be staying on the Goldenrod Trail. At 4.4 miles, the trail seems to end, as it meets a service road. Bear right, and walk the asphalt past the water tank. You'll hook up with the trail again at 4.5 miles. At 4.7 miles, you'll pick up the Buckeye Trail, just before the Goldenrod Trail heads uphill. Take the right onto Buckeye, and you'll find yourself on a fantastically secluded trail along the creek, where you'll pass a bench inviting you to sit for a bit.

Eucalyptus trees tower over Bort Meadow.

Shortly after passing the bench, the trail crosses a second bridge and ends at 5 miles, at the edge of Bort Meadow. Cross this grassy area and look for a junction near the pit toilets. You can walk the paved road, but instead, take the trail marked "Horses OK/No Bikes" to the right of the gate.

At 5.3 miles the trail splits; bear left and continue uphill. At the top of the hill, this trail ends and you'll pick up the MacDonald Trail at 5.4 miles. Turn right and walk a few steps back to the parking area.

66. West Ridge Loop

Round trip: 3.7-mile loop
Hiking time: 4 hours
High point: 1385 feet
Elevation gain: 85 feet
Best hiking time: September through May
Water: From a parking-lot faucet; or bring your own
Map: USGS Oakland East
Contact: East Bay Regional Park District, (510) 562-7275

Getting there: From Highway 24 in Alameda County, exit Highway 13 south. After about 3 miles, exit at Joaquin Miller Road. At the foot of the exit ramp, make a left, then take the next left and go straight onto Joaquin Miller. Drive uphill about 1 mile, then turn left onto Skyline Boulevard (there's a brown parks sign before the turn, and a traffic light). Drive about 3 miles (past the Chabot Space and Science Center), then turn right into the parking lot.

From Highway 24 in Contra Costa County, exit at Fish Ranch Road (if you're driving eastbound on Highway 24, it's the first exit after the tunnel, then stay in the right lane). Drive uphill on Fish Ranch Road about 1 mile, then turn right onto Grizzly Peak Boulevard. Drive 2.4 miles, then turn left onto Skyline Boulevard, drive 2 miles, and turn left into the parking lot. On weekends, there is a fee to park.

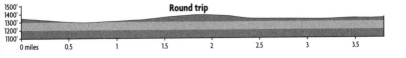

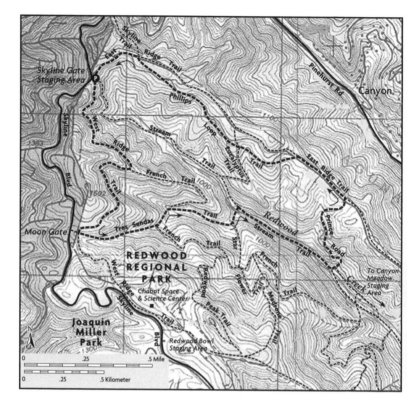

On the drive up, you'll have plenty of opportunity to gaze out on the East Bay, if you can see past all the home construction. But once you reach the large parking area announcing the Redwood Regional Park, breathe a sigh of relief, as you'll soon lose yourself in a forest of redwoods.

Yep, big ol' redwoods, here in the East Bay. Strange, but true. This is a park with a variety of trail choices—all open to leashed dogs—but taking the West Ridge Trail to East Ridge Trail route gets you into the wild the quickest, and it's the prettiest option (my humble opinion).

To start, walk to the south corner of the parking lot, where you can tank up at a faucet, and look for the signed West Ridge Trail. This wide dirt path gets a lot of use, where on clear days you'll be able to see Mount Diablo. At a 0.5 mile, you'll come to a signed trailhead for French Trail; stay on the West Ridge Trail. At 1 mile, turn left onto the Tres Sendas Trail, which is closed to cyclists and offers the chance to get the dogs off-leash. You'll be walking in the shade of the redwoods and through a mix of bay laurel and hazelnut. In the wetter months, this area can get

Redwoods in Oakland? Yes, along the West Ridge Trail.

slick, since the trail crosses a seasonal stream a couple of times. At 1.4 miles, Tres Sendas crosses French Trail, but you'll stay on Tres Sendas (Spanish for "Three Paths.") At 1.7 miles, you'll come to the signed Star Flower Trail, but press on following Tres Sendas.

Just past this junction, you'll meet up with Redwood Creek, where wild trout still spawn. Follow the path as it crosses the creek and joins with the Stream Trail; bear right (bear left and the trail takes you back to the trailhead for a shorter hike).

At 2.2 miles, you'll reach the junction with Prince Road; turn left onto it. This trail heads a bit uphill, where you'll find a bench on which to rest. But the climb doesn't really last that long, as at 2.4 miles the trail ends at a junction with the East Ridge Trail where you'll turn left.

At 2.7 miles, East Ridge Trail meets up with the Philips Loop Trail, where you have the option of returning to the parking area on the relatively flat East Ridge Trail, or you can choose some ups and downs along the Philips Loop Trail. I like the Philips option, since it ends at 3.6 miles with the East Ridge Trail. At that junction, take the East Ridge Trail toward the parking area, noting that the Bay Area Ridge Trail/East Bay Skyline National Recreation Trail breaks off near here and heads north (this 31-mile trail runs from Wildcat Canyon Park near Richmond to Anthony Chabot Park near Castro Valley).

From the East Ridge/Philips Loop junction, it's a short, level hike back to the parking area.

67. Sibley Volcanic Regional Preserve

Round trip: 2.6-mile loop
Hiking time: 1.5 hours
High point: 1400 feet
Elevation gain: 100 feet
Best hiking time: Year-round
Water: At the trailhead
Map: USGS Briones Valley
Contact: East Bay Regional Park District, (510) 562-7275

Getting there: From Highway 24 in Alameda County, exit at Claremont Avenue. Drive 1.5 miles northeast on Claremont Avenue to a major intersection with Ashby Road. Continue straight through the light, and turn right to remain on Claremont Avenue (Claremont Boulevard veers left). You should see a brown parks sign for Tilden and Sibley Parks, then pass the back on the Claremont Hotel on the right. Continue on Claremont about 2 miles to the intersection with Grizzly Peak Boulevard. Turn right and drive about 2.4 miles to the intersection with Skyline Boulevard. Turn left onto Skyline, and almost immediately, after 0.1 mile, turn left into the preserve entrance.

This is a complicated geological area, what with volcanic dikes, mudflows, and lava flows. A eucalyptus forest covers most of the trails in this area, which has a violent past and a calm and comforting future.

The Sibley Volcanic Regional Preserve was one of three initial parks established by the East Bay Regional Park District, way back in 1936. Even farther back, about 10 million years ago, lava flowed through the area, spreading north toward Inspiration Point and southeast to Morgana. Eventually, weather eroded the hard volcanic rock, which is now open for all to see. At the unstaffed visitor center, be sure to pick up the brochure detailing a self-guided trek through this volcanic wonderland.

From the visitor center (where there are bathrooms and water fountains), turn left and continue on the paved road, where you'll gain views toward

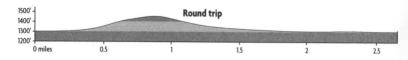

Redwood Regional Park (Hike 66) and the Huckleberry Preserve (where dogs are *not* allowed). After just 0.1 mile, the trail splits at an unsigned junction. Stay on the paved trail leading right. Here, you'll see bay laurel, Monterey pine, and coast live oak.

At 0.3 mile, you'll reach the signed junction with the Round Top Loop Trail; bear right onto this narrow trail. It stays nearly level, then gains elevation slightly, where you'll find a spur road at 0.3 mile. Stay with the Round Top Loop Trail. At 0.8 mile, the trail reaches a junction; walk toward a fenced viewpoint. Here you'll get to see the Round Top volcano. Mining opened the area to basalt extraction and, in that time, a labyrinth appeared at this viewpoint (there are two, one a bit farther on); you'll find small trinkets, coins, and other objects piled in the center of the labyrinths. These are not true mazes, but rather stone-lined paths, which show signs of someone lovingly

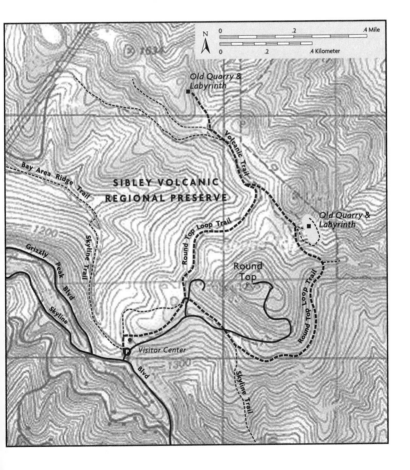

Peaks surround the Sibley Volcanic Regional Preserve.

caring for their upkeep. They are strange and bizarre and worth exploring.

After this first labyrinth, head back to the junction and continue north on the signed Volcanic Trail. At 1.5 miles, you'll reach a junction where there is a water trough; bear right and you'll come to a second junction where you'll go right. There is another labyrinth near here. When you're done exploring it, retrace your steps to the junction to regain the Round Top Loop Trail, at 1.9 miles.

At 2.3 miles, you'll reach a multiple-trail junction, where you started your loop around Round Top. Turn right to return to the parking area.

68. Nimitz Way

Round trip: 7-mile loop
Hiking time: 3–5 hours
High point: 1211 feet
Elevation gain: 800 feet
Best hiking time: Year-round
Water: At the trailhead
Map: USGS Briones Valley
Contact: East Bay Regional Park District, (510) 562-7275

Getting there: From Highway 24 in the East Bay, drive to just east of the Caldecott Tunnel and take the Fish Ranch Road exit, then go northeast to

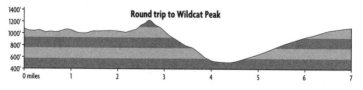

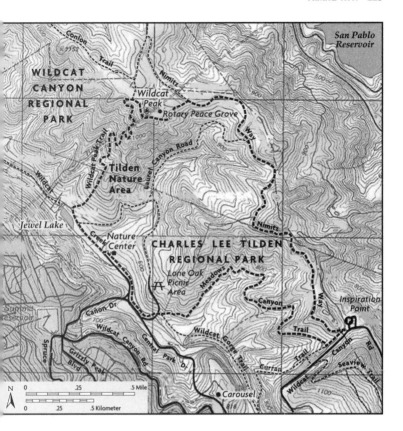

Grizzly Peak Boulevard. Turn right, drive up the hill, and turn right again on South Park Drive. Drive 1 mile to the Wildcat Canyon Road, stay to the right, and drive to the signed parking area at Inspiration Point. It should be noted that South Park Drive is closed from November to March to allow for the migration of protected newts. To avoid South Park Drive, from Highway 24 drive through the Caldecott Tunnel and exit at Orinda. Turn left on Camino Pablo. Drive north about 2 miles, turn left on Wildcat Canyon Road, and continue to Inspiration Point on your right.

On this hike, each new twist in the trail brings on new—and jaw-dropping—views of the San Pablo Reservoir, the East Bay, and the grassy East Bay hillsides. Go on a clear day, when Wildcat Peak calls out to be climbed.

The hike rests within the Charles Lee Tilden Regional Park, one of three original East Bay Regional Park District parks opened to the public in 1936. It was named after Major Charles Lee Tilden, a park founder

A hike along Nimitz Way offers a variety of views.

and the first president of the park district's board of directors.

The hike starts at the gated Nimitz Way road, dedicated to the World War II admiral. This paved trail is part—some say the prettiest—of the Bay Area Ridge Trail/East Bay Skyline Trail. The first 2 miles stay fairly level on this wide trail. You'll see plenty of dog walkers, hikers, and cyclists, so heed the signs and stay to the right. You'll get on-and-off views of Mount Diablo to the southeast, San Pablo Reservoir to the east, and San Francisco Bay to the west (on clear days, the Bay Bridge is quite photogenic).

Two slim paths lead from Nimitz Way and climb west to put you on top of Wildcat Peak in just 0.5 mile of strolling. At the top, take a break at the Peace Grove platform and do a 360-degree search for San Francisco landmarks like Mount Tamalpais and Angel Island.

From here, pick up the Wildcat Peak Trail southwest down to a duck pond called Jewel Lake at 3.7 miles. At most times of the year, the lake is filled with waterfowl, so be sure to have tight control on your dog. Continue on the Wildcat Peak Trail southwest, where you'll walk along a paved road for nearly 0.5 mile to the Lone Oak Picnic Area (a good place to stop for a snack) and then pick up the Meadows Canyon Trail at 5.4 miles. Here's where you'll encounter the bulk of the climbing on this hike. Still, it's gradual, as the trail stays just above a tributary of Wildcat Creek for 0.7 mile. Note that you'll be moving through a narrow, grassy strip, framed by giant bay laurel and coast live oaks.

When you reach the Curran Trail at 6.8 miles, take a left to pass through a fragrant eucalyptus grove leading toward the trailhead.

69. San Pablo Ridge Trail

Round trip: 6-mile loop
Hiking time: 3 hours
High point: 1057 feet
Elevation gain: 1200 feet
Best hiking time: Year-round; but pretty hot in the summer
Water: At the trailhead
Map: USGS Richmond
Contact: East Bay Regional Park District, (510) 562-7275

Getting there: From eastbound Interstate 80 in Contra Costa County, take the Solano exit. At the base of the ramp, turn left onto Amador Avenue, drive 0.4 mile, and turn right onto McBryde Avenue. Move into the left lane, and after about 0.3 mile, at the stop sign, continue straight onto Park Avenue. Drive 0.1 mile, turn left into the park, and continue a short distance to the Alvarado Staging Area at the end of the road.

From westbound I-80 in Contra Costa County, exit at McBryde. Turn left (east) on McBryde and after crossing over the highway, get into the left lane of McBryde and proceed as above.

OK, you're new to the Bay Area and you're wondering, "Where is the wildest place I can get to where even the thought of civilization will melt away?" Try Wildcat Canyon Regional Park just east of Richmond. You'll be amazed how quickly you can get back into the grassy canyons, where deer, coyote, bobcat, and all manner of birds roam and flit around.

This park, now at 2440 acres, has a history to match its wildness. Here's what the East Bay Regional Park District has to say:

> *On a spring day in 1772 Pedro Fages, Fray Juan Crespi and a 'small band of six Catalonian volunteers' entered a Native American village located near the mouth of Wildcat Creek. Although their search for a trade route north had been frustrated by the broad, swift waters of the*

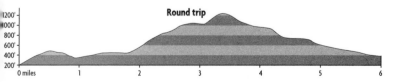

Carquinez Straits, they found the native people to be welcoming. Fages traded glass beads for food and tools. In his diary he refers to his hosts as 'peaceful heathens.' These Native Americans did not practice agriculture since they were able to identify and gather a great variety of edible and medicinal plants. They hunted deer and elk and took fish, clams, mussels and oysters from the Bay.

In 1935 the East Bay Regional Park District acquired the southern part of Wildcat Canyon to create Charles Lee Tilden Regional Park. In 1952 the northern part was sold by East Bay Municipal Utility District to private interests. Standard Oil drilled exploratory wells there in 1966, but the results did not justify further drilling. In 1967 the Park District bought an initial 400 acres, and by 1976 the District owned enough land to form a 2,197-acre Regional Park.

This 6-mile loop takes you from a starting point at 180 feet to the top of San Pablo Ridge at 1057 feet. Start on the paved Wildcat Creek Trail, which climbs from the parking lot in an easy grade. At 2 miles, you'll meet up with the Mezue Trail, where you'll take a left. After crossing a cattle gate, you'll begin to climb again, but the views will keep you going. As you continue to climb, you'll think the ridge is within reach, but

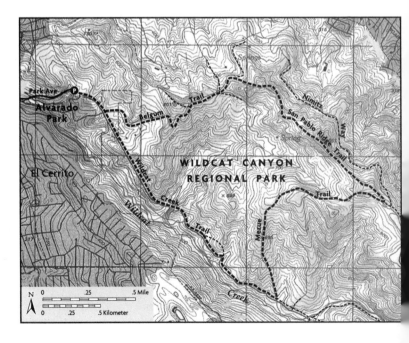

San Pablo Reservoir from San Pablo Ridge.

the trail dips right and you'll lose ground until you get to the junction with the San Pablo Ridge Trail at 3.3 miles.

Turning left on San Pablo Ridge Trail, notice the hawks and turkey vultures that soar on the thermals. Finally, you'll reach the high point of the trek, a nifty spot to take a rest and tank up on water (be sure to bring plenty for your dog, too).

At 4.5 miles, San Pablo Ridge Trail ends at a signed junction. Stay straight, where you'll find yourself on the Belgum Trail. This trail makes an easy, sweep downhill, and you'll pass an old settlement (the palm trees look out of place). The Belgum Trail meets up with the Wildcat Creek Trail at 5.5 miles. Turn right and retrace this paved trail back to the parking area.

70. Laurel Loop

Round trip: 3-mile loop
Hiking time: 1.5 hours
High point: 550 feet
Elevation gain: 300 feet
Best hiking time: Year-round
Water: At the trailhead
Maps: USGS Richmond
Contact: East Bay Regional Park District, (510) 562-7275

Getting there: From Interstate 80 in Contra Costa County, exit at San Pablo Dam Road. Drive southeast on San Pablo Dam Road (toward El

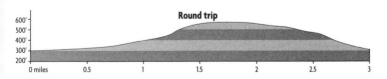

It's an easy hike among the eucalyptus at the Kennedy Grove Regional Park.

Sobrante) about 4.5 miles (about 0.6 mile past Castro Ranch Road), and turn left into Kennedy Grove Regional Park. Continue about 0.2 mile to the park entrance kiosk. When the kiosk is staffed (usually on weekends and holidays), it costs $4 to park.

Not all hikes have to be killers. In a world fraught with stress, it's good to have places where you can chill, take a leisurely stroll, and end up

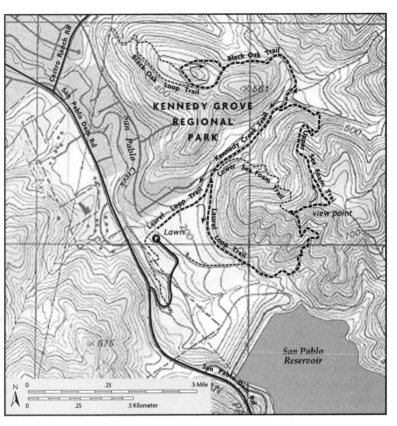

joining a pick-up game of football while your dog watches from the sidelines. Kennedy Grove Regional Park is just such a place.

The park is a destination point on weekends for picnics, weddings, and games of all sorts in a wide, grassy area at the center of the park (dogs must be leashed here, but can be off-leash and under voice command in the undeveloped areas of the park). You'll find picnic tables, barbecue pits, a playground area, and volleyball and horseshoe pits. Sadly, some people never leave the eucalyptus-lined grassy area, but this 3-mile loop will take you through the 218-acre park in style.

Pick up a paved walking trail at the overflow parking area near the kiosk. At about two-thirds of the way through the parking area, pick up the Laurel Loop Trail at the gate. This multiuse trail climbs slightly past an off-limits service road, then crests at a junction, where you'll bear right. Ignore the path heading uphill to the left and continue around the hill toward a junction at 0.4 mile, where you'll make a left. This trail is closed to cyclists and offers the first place where you can let your dog off the leash.

At 0.7 mile, you'll meet up with the Upper Sea Foam Trail, where you'll bear right. The trail continues uphill to a bench that offers great views of San Pablo Reservoir. After a steep but blessedly short grade, Upper Sea Foam drops into a canyon, then rises and falls to a junction at 1.4 miles. Here, you'll turn right onto the Black Oak Trail, a wide, multiuse trail that crosses a creek. At 1.75 miles, the trail splits at a signed junction; you'll want to bear left. The path levels out, then completes a loop.

After a short stretch through a grassy area, the trail reaches an area that features a picnic table and makes for a nice rest stop. After a bit, begin your descent through black oak and coast live oak. At 2.1 miles, you'll reach yet another junction; turn right to go back to the junction with the Upper Sea Foam Trail. At 2.5 miles, pick up the Kennedy Creek Trail, where at 2.7 miles, the trail meets up with the Laurel Loop Trail. Bear right as the trail takes you to the bulk of the action in Kennedy Grove.

71. Sobrante Ridge Trail

Round trip: 2.5 miles
Hiking time: 1 hour
High point: 750 feet
Elevation gain: 330 feet
Best hiking time: Year-round
Water: At the trailhead
Map: USGS Briones Valley
Contact: East Bay Regional Park District, (510) 562-7275

Getting there: From Interstate 80 in Contra Costa County, exit at San Pablo Dam Road. Drive about 3.5 miles southeast on San Pablo Dam Road to the traffic light at Castro Ranch Road. Turn left and drive about 0.8 mile, then turn left (into a housing development) on Conestoga Way. Drive uphill about 0.3 mile, turn left onto Carriage Drive, drive about

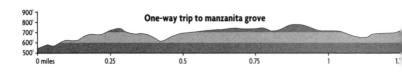

A new subdivision fills the valley below Sobrante Ridge.

0.2 mile, and then turn right onto Coach Drive. Take Coach Drive about 0.3 mile to the park entrance at the end of the cul-de-sac.

If there's one hike in the Bay Area that shows how important the East Bay Regional Park system is, this might be it. *Sobrante* in Spanish means leftover, or surplus, but this area is anything but a scrap of land. Nope, this is prime real estate, a 277-acre island that's wedged between look-alike housing developments (top the ridge and that's all you can see).

The land provided a vital link for the East Bay Municipal Utility District's watershed lands, as well as for the rest of the East Bay Regional Parks. A wide variety of animals, from raptors and songbirds to deer and coyote, use this land as a migration corridor. The botanical preserve is also the home of one of the last stands of Alameda manzanita, a rare and endangered chaparral plant. A miniature forest of manzanita clings to the grassy hillsides in soil so barren that nothing else grows. The manzanita survives by sucking up moisture from the frequent fog that spills over the ridge.

Pick up the trail at the small parking area and start uphill (it's a leg stretcher), cross under the high-tension powerlines, and come to a gate

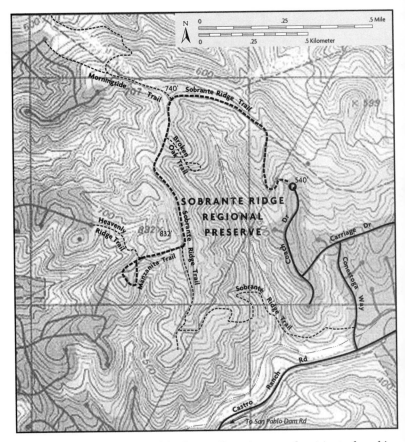

at 0.2 mile. Go straight and find your first views, and not just of cookie-cutter housing developments. On a clear day, expect to see San Pablo Bay and Mount Diablo. The trail shrinks from a road to a trail here, and in the summer it bakes hard; you'll likely see rattlesnakes sunning themselves. It's best to keep your dogs under control, lest they get poked in the nose by a disturbed rattler.

At 0.6 mile, you'll reach the junction with the Morningside Trail; stay on the Sobrante Ridge Trail, where you'll find yourself on part of the Bay Area Ridge Trail (when completed, the trail will circle San Francisco Bay). The trail continues south, to the first of the preserve's picnic tables. At 0.7 miles, you'll reach the junction with the Broken Oak Trail. Stay straight, where you'll dip into a forest of bay laurel and coast live oak (be sure to watch for bobcat footprints on the dusty trail).

At 1.1 miles, take a right onto Manzanita Trail, which drops sharply near the edge of a housing development. At 1.2 miles, the trail splits, but you'll stay to the right. Here, you'll get your first look at the Alameda manzanita, but they're still spread out among the coast live oaks. You'll soon reach a grove and an interpretive sign that explains the plight of the manzanita, where the plants literally crowd the trail.

The trail crests a hill, passes a giant madrone tree, and drops back down to a junction at 1.3 miles. From here, you'll retrace your steps back down to the parking area.

72. Briones Crest

Round trip: 5.6-mile loop
Hiking time: 3.5 hours
High point: 1483 feet
Elevation gain: 1300 feet
Best hiking time: Spring; hikable year-round
Water: At the trailhead
Map: USGS Briones Valley; park map from kiosk
Contact: East Bay Regional Park District, (510) 562-7275

Getting there: From Interstate 680 north of Pleasant Hill, take Highway 4 west for 3 miles to the Alhambra Avenue exit. Turn south on Alhambra Avenue and drive 0.5 mile, where you'll bear right onto Alhambra Valley Road. Drive another mile to Reliez Valley Road. Turn right and follow Reliez Valley Road 0.5 mile to the park entrance (there are stables there). Turn right and drive 0.5 mile to the parking area (when the kiosk is staffed, usually on weekends and holidays, it costs $4 to park).

East Bay regulars rate this 5700-acre park as the best of the bunch in the East Bay Regional Park system. With places to hike, bike, and ride horses, it's no wonder this park gets a lot of use. Well, no one said you didn't have to conform; come on, join the crowds and see how this park's

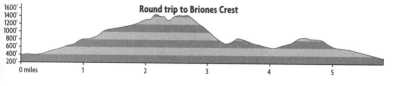

Round trip to Briones Crest

The trail is wide and inviting heading toward Briones Crest.

network of trails can take you to places where you'll swear no one else has stood.

There's a host of trail junctions on this loop, so it's best to pick up a free map at the kiosk in the parking lot and match it up with a good topo map.

From the gate near the information kiosk, start on the Alhambra Creek Trail. This is a typical East Bay trek—plenty of grasslands with valley oaks standing guard—but as you gain elevation on the Alhambra Creek Trail, you'll be greeted in the spring by the most dazzling wildflower display I've ever found. California poppies, buttercups, lupine, and clover cover the landscape.

At 1 mile, you'll come to the junction with the Spengler Trail, where you'll make a right and start climbing away from the creek. At 1.6 miles, you'll reach two treeless ponds (they're fenced off to keep the cattle out) called the Maricich Lagoons. Here, you'll turn left onto the Old Briones Road Trail. Climb gradually along more grassy knolls, then bear left onto Briones Crest Trail at 1.9 miles.

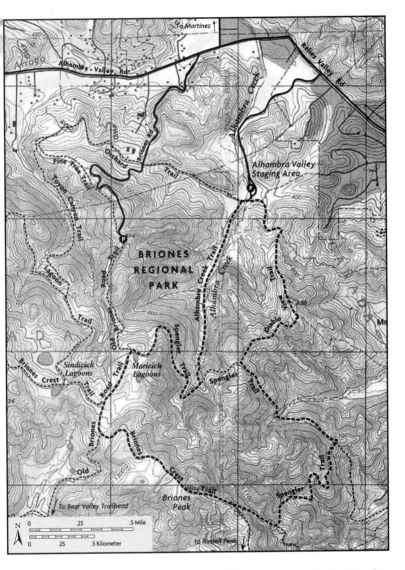

This stretch of trail takes you up to 1483-foot Briones Peak. It's a leg killer, gaining much elevation in just 2.5 miles. The sweat you just spilt was worth it, as this is the highest peak in the entire park and grants a panoramic view of the East Bay's rolling hillsides.

To complete the loop, turn left on the Spengler Trail, then take a right onto the Diablo View Trail, which you'll follow down to the parking area in another 1.1 miles.

73. Lafayette Ridge

Round trip: 4.5 miles
Hiking time: 4 hours
High point: 1400 feet
Elevation gain: 1300 feet
Best hiking time: Year-round
Water: Bring your own
Map: USGS Briones Valley
Contact: East Bay Regional Park District, (510) 562-7275

Getting there: From Highway 24 just west of Walnut Creek, take the Pleasant Hill Road exit. Drive north for about a mile and then make a U-turn at Reliez Valley Road. Double back on Pleasant Hill Road for 0.2 mile and park for free at the large Lafayette Staging Area.

The 6002-acre Briones Regional Park has four major access points that lead to all sorts of trail loops. This hike is not one of those. Nope, this trek takes you from the parking area just off the road up Lafayette Ridge Trail to its terminus at the Russell Peak Trail, giving you the option to extend this trek all the way to Russell Peak and back.

I like this trip because it gets you into views quickly. From the ridgeline, you'll likely see hawks (notably, redtail hawks and the occasional golden eagle) and turkey vultures soaring, and jays and red-shouldered blackbirds will likely call to you from the scrub.

Pick up the trail past a gate and head up the grassy hillside (in spring it's awash with wild radish and mustard). This shadeless portion can bake you well-done in the summer, but it does offer great views of Mount Diablo and Las Trampas Ridge. Catch the wildflower explosion in the spring, when you'll see California poppy, chamomile, and fiddleneck in a showy display.

At 0.6 mile, you'll pass a boarded-up structure, an old farmhouse

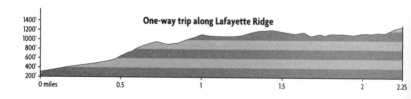

One-way trip along Lafayette Ridge

On the way to Lafayette Ridge, be on the lookout for hawks and soaring turkey vultures.

that must have been something in its day. About 100 yards farther, there's an unsigned junction, but you'll want to continue on the Lafayette Ridge Trail, where you'll pass a grove of evergreen bay laurel and coast live oak. This stretch features the most strenuous climbing, but push on.

At 1 mile, pass a gate next to a grove of eucalyptus, wipe the sweat from your brow and enjoy some level walking. The trail turns to single-track, just wide enough for one person to pass, and you'll enter a forest of coast live oak. After a rainstorm, try searching for bobcat, deer, and coyote tracks left behind in the soft mud.

You'll come to the end of the trail at 2.25 miles, where you can either push to the top of Russell Peak (in just more than 0.6 mile, making for a 5.8-mile round trip), or take a breather on top of the ridge and retrace your steps back down to the trailhead.

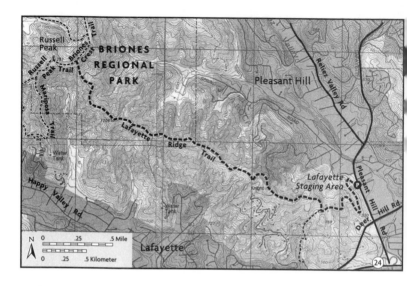

74. Franklin Ridge

Round trip: 3.4-mile loop
Hiking time: 3 hours
High point: 650 feet
Elevation gain: 1200 feet
Best hiking time: Year-round
Water: Bring your own
Map: USGS Benicia
Contact: East Bay Regional Park District, (510) 562-7275

Getting there: From Highway 4 in Contra Costa County, exit at Alhambra Avenue. Drive north on Alhambra about 2 miles, then turn left (at a stop sign) onto Escobar Street. Drive about 0.1 mile, then turn right onto Talbart Street. Drive on Talbart (which becomes Carquinez Scenic Drive) about 0.3 mile, then turn left into the Nejedly Staging Area.

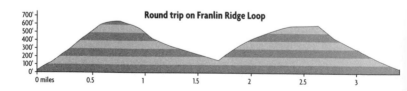

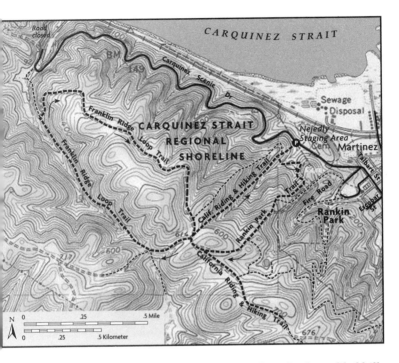

What, another hike through the rolling grasslands and oak-studded hill-sides of the East Bay? Well, sure. Remember, you're in East Bay Regional Park District territory, where one park can look just like another. Still, open space is open space, and this park system is dog-friendly, so you might as well enjoy what they have to offer.

And this hike, on the east side of the Carquinez Strait Regional Shoreline near Martinez (where hiker extraordinaire John Muir was born), offers something the others can't—exceptional views of the strait, which is the gateway to the San Joaquin Delta. You'll be hiking up and down and up and down, but there are enough benches and rest stops for gazing out onto the choppy, frothy, olive-brown waters of the strait. From the top of Franklin Ridge, you'll also see Mount Diablo, Mount Tamalpais, as well as ships passing under the Interstate 680 bridge.

The trek starts with a choice of three trails, which are all pretty steep. You'll want to take the gated Rankin Park Trail, which starts next to a picnic table under an oak. The trail soon forks at a cattle gate, but stay to the left. Continue up Rankin Park Trail (you'll come to your first bench at 0.2 mile) and reach the California Riding and Hiking Trail at 0.7 mile; turn right.

This trail—open to hikers, mountain bikers, and horse riders—descends

The city of Martinez, where John Muir was born, from Franklin Ridge.

slightly to the junction with the Franklin Ridge Loop Trail at 0.8 mile. Turn left onto Franklin Ridge, where you'll gain access to views of Grizzly Bay, Suisun Bay, and the towns of Benicia and Martinez.

Continue clockwise and, at 1.75 miles, a spur trail continues straight to link up with Carquinez Scenic Drive, but veer right and continue on the Franklin Ridge Loop Trail. Here, you'll gain a lot of the elevation eventually lost, as this stretch rises through gnarled, but stately, oaks. At a little more than 1.9 miles, look for an unsigned trail that goes left. It leads to a bench with great views at 2 miles, making for a good lunch spot; but in summer the star thistle nearly takes over, and this plant can really do a number on you dog's nose.

Retrace your steps back to the Franklin Ridge Loop Trail and turn left. At 2.2 miles, you'll reach an unsigned junction, but stay straight. At 2.75 miles, there's another junction, but stay straight again. At nearly 3 miles, you'll reach the last dead-end trail junction, and yes, continue straight a few short steps until you get to the signed junction for the California Hiking and Riding Trail, where you'll turn left. At 3.4 miles, the trail ends at the gate of the parking lot.

75. Murietta Falls

Round trip: 11.5 miles
Hiking time: 8 hours
High point: 3300 feet
Elevation gain: 3500 feet
Best hiking time: September through June
Water: Bring plenty of your own
Map: USGS Mendenhall Springs
Contact: East Bay Regional Park District, (510) 562-7275

Getting there: From Interstate 580 in Livermore, take the North Livermore Avenue exit and turn right. Drive south for 3.5 miles (the road becomes Tesla Road) to Mines Road. Turn right on Mines Road and drive 3.5 miles to Del Valle Road. Continue on Del Valle Road for another 3 miles until you come to the Del Valle Regional Park entrance. Drive less than a mile to the dam at Del Valle Reservoir, cross it, turn right, and drive 0.5 mile to the Lichen Bark Picnic Area and Campground and the trailhead for the Ohlone Trail. Parking is $6 and a wilderness permit is $2, with a $1 fee for bringing your dog in.

Psssssst: wanna know where the tallest waterfall in the Bay Area is? Right at the end of this hike, that's where.

Murietta Falls plummets some 100 feet down slick, moss-covered granite and makes for a nifty spot to take a dip in the numerous small pools. The falls, located inside the Ohlone Regional Wilderness, are named for Joaquin Murietta, a noted outlaw who rode this area in the 1800s.

Quite frankly, there's no other destination like this one in the Bay Area. Hit it right—when the stream is free-flowing and the falls are a pounding fountain of froth—and you'll be rewarded. Hit it wrong—don't even

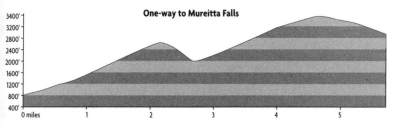

One-way to Mureitta Falls

try it in July, when the falls just trickle—and the only thing you'll get is a hardy workout.

Yep, this hike in a butt kicker. It's 5.75 miles one way and sticks to a steep, rocky ridgeline that gains and loses elevation. In fact, on one stretch of the Ohlone Trail, you'll gain 1600 feet in 1.5 miles of hiking (it's truly the worst part). So be prepared.

But get this: it's one place in the Bay Area where you can actually take a decent backpacking trip (alas, sans dogs; the park is only open to pooches in the daylight hours). This is rugged country, where you have the chance

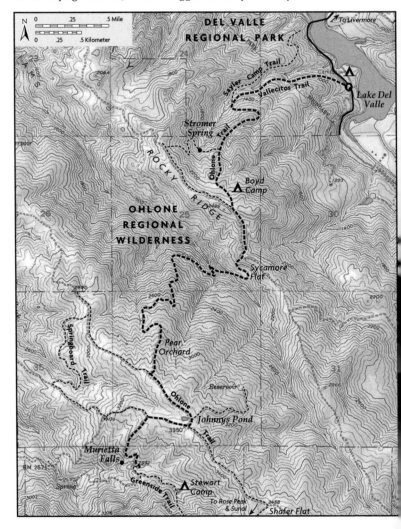

Murietta Falls, early spring (photo by Marc Soares)

to see bald eagles, mountain lions, coyotes, bobcats, deer and a herd of majestic tule elk.

The route tops out on Rocky Ridge at 2.3 miles, drops 500 feet in 0.5 mile, and then climbs another 1200 feet to Wauhab Ridge. You'll reach Johnnys Pond at 4.7 miles. Turn right at the junction with Springboard Trail (marker 35); from here, it's a mile hike to the falls.

Trek along the ridge for 0.25 mile, then turn left onto the Greenside Trail, which will take you on a sharp descent to the gulch where the falls remain hidden. You can't really get a good look from this trail, so you'll need to find the unsigned path that takes you past the creek to actually get into the floor of the canyon, where the water flows down rocky points into a large pool.

Since this hike takes some time to complete (and you need to get your dog out before the sun sets), it's best not to linger too long at the falls. Just retrace your steps back out to the Ohlone Trail (the trail is very well marked) and remember to be careful as you make your way back down the rocky ridge.

APPENDIX: RESOURCES

Books

Mullally, Linda. *Hiking with Dogs: Becoming a Wilderness-Wise Dog Owner*. Missoula, MT: Falcon Guides, 1999.

Soares, Marc. *100 Hikes in the San Francisco Bay Area*. Seattle: The Mountaineers Books, 2001.

————*75 Year-Round Hikes in Northern California*, Seattle: The Mountaineers Books, 2000.

Stienstra, Tom, and Ann Marie Brown. *California Hiking*. Emeryville, CA: Foghorn Press, 2003.

Hiking and Dog-Related Websites

Bay Area Backcountry, *www.hknot.com/bab/bab.html.*

Bay Area Hiker, "Where to Take My Dog," *www.bahiker.com/doghikes.html.*

East Bay Regional Park District, *www.ebparks.org.*

Peninsula Access for Dogs, *www.prusik.com/pads.*

First Aid

Acker, Randy, DVM. *Dog First Aid: A Field Guide to Emergency Care for the Outdoor Dog*. Gallatin Gateway, MT: Wilderness Adventure Press, 1999. Dr. Acker also offers a comprehensive dog first-aid kit containing most of the items listed in this book's introduction, all packaged in a convenient fanny pack. For information, contact him at the Sun Valley Animal Center, (800) 699-2663 or online at *www.svanimal.com.*

Ruffwear Inc. offers prepackaged dog first-aid kits containing the essentials. The packets are available at many outdoor retail shops, or order directly from Ruffwear online at *www.ruffwear.com.*

Dog Gear

Cascade Designs Inc. *(www.cascadedesigns.com)* invented the inflatable sleeping pad for hikers thirty years ago and now offers a line of fleece-covered pads just for dogs.

Granite Gear *(www.granitegear.com)* offers a full line of backpacks for your dog.

Planetdog *(www.planetdog.com)* makes active gear for your pet, including toys, packable bowls, beds, leashes, leads, and collars. The company donates a portion of its profits to environmental charities.

Ruffwear Inc. *(www.ruffwear.com)* offers a full line of dog accessories for the active dog. The company makes the popular (and well-worth-the-price) booties for rough environments.

Even in the urban setting of San Francisco, hikers and their dogs can find pockets of rustic wilderness.

INDEX

ABOUT THE AUTHOR

Thom Gabrukiewicz is the outdoor editor/writer for the *Record Searchlight*, Redding, California's daily newspaper. Gabrukiewicz's weekly Outdoors section was judged best in the nation by the Outdoor Writers Association of America in 2003 and 2004. Gabrukiewicz also was named California Outdoor Writer of the Year in 2003 by the Outdoor Writers Association of California. He lives in Redding with his wife, Sharon, and children Jessica and Cody, along with the girls, Scully and Trinity.

THE MOUNTAINEERS, founded in 1906, is a nonprofit outdoor activity and conservation club, whose mission is "to explore, study, preserve, and enjoy the natural beauty of the outdoors. . . . " Based in Seattle, Washington, the club is now the third-largest such organization in the United States, with seven branches throughout Washington State.

The Mountaineers sponsors both classes and year-round outdoor activities in the Pacific Northwest, which include hiking, mountain climbing, ski-touring, snowshoeing, bicycling, camping, kayaking and canoeing, nature study, sailing, and adventure travel. The club's conservation division supports environmental causes through educational activities, sponsoring legislation, and presenting informational programs. All club activities are led by skilled, experienced volunteers, who are dedicated to promoting safe and responsible enjoyment and preservation of the outdoors.

If you would like to participate in these organized outdoor activities or the club's programs, consider a membership in The Mountaineers. For information and an application, write or call The Mountaineers, Club Headquarters, 300 Third Avenue West, Seattle, Washington 98119; 206-284-6310.

The Mountaineers Books, an active, nonprofit publishing program of the club, produces guidebooks, instructional texts, historical works, natural history guides, and works on environmental conservation. All books produced by The Mountaineers fulfill the club's mission.

Send or call for our catalog of more than 500 outdoor titles:

The Mountaineers Books
1001 SW Klickitat Way, Suite 201
Seattle, WA 98134
800-553-4453
mbooks@mountaineersbooks.org
www.mountaineersbooks.org

The Mountaineers Books is proud to be a corporate sponsor of The Leave No Trace Center for Outdoor Ethics, whose mission is to promote and inspire responsible outdoor recreation through education, research, and partnerships. The Leave No Trace program is focused specifically on human-powered (nonmotorized) recreation.

Leave No Trace strives to educate visitors about the nature of their recreational impacts, as well as offer techniques to prevent and minimize such impacts. Leave No Trace is best understood as an educational and ethical program, not as a set of rules and regulations.

For more information, visit *www.LNT.org*, or call 800-332-4100.

OTHER TITLES YOU MIGHT ENJOY FROM THE MOUNTAINEERS BOOKS:

BEST HIKES WITH CHILDREN:
San Francisco Bay Area, 2nd Edition
Bill & Kevin McMillon
Explore more than 2000 miles of easy trails in the
diverse Bay area.

100 HIKES IN THE SAN FRANCISCO BAY AREA
Marc Soares
The ultimate weekend or after-work get-aways,
within easy reach of Bay Area cities.

100 CLASSIC HIKES IN NORTHERN CALIFORNIA,
John & Marc Soares
A full-color guide to the best hikes in Northern
California.

DON'T FORGET THE DUCT TAPE:
Tips and Tricks for Repairing Outdoor Gear,
Kristin Hostetter
Pack this little guide with you and be an
outdoor fixit guru!

WATERFALL LOVER'S GUIDE TO NORTHERN
CALIFORNIA: More than 300 Waterfalls from the
North Coast to the Southern Sierra
Matt & Krissi Danielsson
A comprehensive field guide to viewing more than 300 waterfalls
in northern California

ALSO IN THE BEST HIKES WITH DOGS SERIES

Colorado, *Ania Savage*
Las Vegas & Beyond, *Kimberly Lewis*
& Paula Jacoby-Garrett
Western Washington, *Dan A. Nelson*
Oregon, *Ellen Morris Bishop*
Arizona, *Renée Guillory*

**Mountaineers Books has more than
500 outdoor recreation titles in print.**
Receive a free catalog at
www.mountaineersbooks.org.